"Sweeney contributes somethi[...] [...]n
the discourse surrounding Mo[...] [...]nd
context. It is refreshing to final[...] [...] of Mother Teresa's
full humanity—her complexity a[...] her sainthood. Sweeney captures
the life and spirituality of one of the most influential religious voices of
the twentieth century, refusing to reduce reflections on her inner life to
clichés and platitudes."

> —Emilie Grosvenor, PhD Candidate, Centre for the Study of
> Religion and Politics, St. Mary's College, University of
> St. Andrews

"A superb brief introduction to the most important saint of our time."

> —James Martin, SJ, author of *Learning to Pray* and *In All Seasons,
> For All Reasons*

People of God

Remarkable Lives, Heroes of Faith

People of God is a series of inspiring biographies for the general reader. Each volume offers a compelling and honest narrative of the life of an important twentieth- or twenty-first-century Catholic. Some living and some now deceased, each of these women and men has known challenges and weaknesses familiar to most of us but responded to them in ways that call us to our own forms of heroism. Each offers a credible and concrete witness of faith, hope, and love to people of our own day.

Teresa of Calcutta

Dark Night, Active Love

Jon M. Sweeney

LITURGICAL PRESS
Collegeville, Minnesota

www.litpress.org

Cover design by Red+Company. Cover illustration by Philip Bannister.

© 2022 by Jon M. Sweeney
Published by Liturgical Press, Collegeville, Minnesota. All rights reserved.
No part of this book may be used or reproduced in any manner whatsoever,
except brief quotations in reviews, without written permission of Liturgical
Press, Saint John's Abbey, PO Box 7500, Collegeville, MN 56321-7500.
Printed in the United States of America.

1	2	3	4	5	6	7	8	9

Library of Congress Control Number: 2022934166

ISBN 978-0-8146-6615-9   978-0-8146-6639-5 (e-book)

If we pray, we will believe.
If we believe, we will love.
If we love, we will serve.

—St. Teresa of Calcutta

Contents

Introduction

Most human beings living in the last quarter of the twentieth century knew Mother Teresa by name and appearance. Most people on the planet could identify her as the saint of the gutters of Calcutta. She was regularly named as one of the most recognized and influential people in the world. International polls ranked her beside Billy Graham as one of the most popular religious figures. *Good Housekeeping* magazine, in 1980, had her atop their list of the world's "most admired women," an honor captured the previous year by the singer, antigay rights activist, and Evangelical Christian Anita Bryant. Two years after her death, she topped a CNN/USA Today Gallup Poll as "the most admired person of the century" ahead of Dr. Martin Luther King Jr., President John F. Kennedy, Albert Einstein, and Helen Keller.[1]

So, what really is there still to say about her? Quite a bit, as it turns out. The stories of both her public and private lives remain little known. We also continue to grapple with the extraordinary things she did, as well as the way that she interpreted the vocation of any would-be follower of Jesus.

Perhaps not quite as universally familiar as it was when she was alive, her striking physical appearance remains vivid in the memories of those who were adults then. It always included the sari—the traditional outer garment of women of the Indian subcontinent—that she'd chosen as the religious uniform of the congregation she founded in 1950: simple white cotton bordered with three blue stripes. She had apparently purchased the first ones "off the rack" at a Calcutta market, the blue edges suggesting to her the Virgin Mary.[2]

She was small in stature, but fiercely strong and always determined. Do an internet search and you will find not a single photograph of her appearing weary, winded, or (outside of moments of prayer) at rest. Yet when we saw her ubiquitous face or watched her at work with children and the dying—which was easy to do, since she was the first great saint in the era of ubiquitous television—we had no idea of the things going on within her that we would learn after her death.

Her surroundings in Calcutta were central to her life and her story. Images of the women, men, and children of that city's streets were familiar. They lay there, destitute, malnourished, and very much alone, even if they were lying near others. Then a tiny woman in a white and blue sari and sandals would bend over to greet them, one by one. She reached out a hand and touched an arm or a shoulder. That is St. Teresa of Calcutta, or "Mother Teresa," as the world still most often remembers her, making her daily rounds.

Other things become clear if you study the photographs or look closely at the videos and documentaries. She had large hands for a woman her size. Mother Teresa was tiny. She stood a mere five feet tall in sandals. For comparison, the diminutive Gandhi was five feet five inches. Her hands were thick, coarse, working hands, and she was a hugger, particularly with infants and toddlers. She would pull children tightly to her cheek, one arm underneath the torso, the other propping up the neck, the way a natural mother holds a child. A joyous smile was common on her face. She used to instruct her fellow Missionaries of Charity, "When I see someone sad, I always think, she is refusing something to Jesus."[3] Yet she was a serious saint, fiercely dedicated to living her calling, and the same face that bore easy smiles was also marked often by a furrowed brow and pursed determination around the lips.

The images are difficult to forget and easy to find, and her story is so well known that we don't really know her.

Mother Teresa died in 1997. When the United Nations Secretary General Javier Perez de Cuellar introduced Mother Teresa before the organization's general assembly, he called her "the most powerful woman in the world."[4] When she traveled to County Mayo, Ireland, to speak at the Marian shrine in Knock in June 1993, Archbishop Joseph Cassidy introduced her by saying, "I'm not being facetious and I'm certainly making no comparison when I say that no woman has made such an impact here since Our Lady herself appeared in 1879."[5] And in her last decades, there were photographs of her and framed quotations by her on the walls of the very Home for the Dying in Calcutta where she lived and worked every day. That must have been strange: to minister with such selflessness while surrounded by images of your own fame.

Active Love, Dark Night

To the intuitive sensibility of the Catholic faithful, Mother Teresa is revered, and her role as an advocate in heaven unquestioned, in the way that only a few other saints of the twentieth century, such as Therese of Lisieux and Padre Pio, have been regarded. She holds a unique distinction, however, as the first great saint of the television age. We came to know her through electronically and digitally transmitted video images, and as such, we felt we knew her in a way that we could not have known any of the saints before her. Through television, we made sense of Mother Teresa, often in real time. The inspiration she took from the words of St. Therese of Lisieux, to be little for God, became more powerful when we saw it—and we saw it often—in action.

We were aware of her activities and movement and influence, as well as the immense compassion she gave to those whom she aided. All of this was more vivid and immediate to people around the globe through the powerful communications technology of the day. Television has "made" saints in ways not unlike how they were made in the premodern era, when popular acclaim among the *populus Dei* is what often determined canonical status: the people of God simply demanded it. In Mother's case (and we will often refer to her simply as "Mother"), prayers for her intercession—if we had statistics for such things—probably outstripped every other saint before her by a multiple of ten. For all of these reasons, in contrast to many earlier biographies of her, I will often be using televised interviews and video accounts as sources to tell her story.

One other aspect of this short biography that is perhaps different from others you have read or seen is an awareness of the significant role of the *other* most important Catholic of the twentieth century, Pope John Paul II, in shaping the Mother Teresa we came to know. His fatherly presence in her life, his own ubiquity in the global communications media, his devotion to the promotion of living embodiments of faith, and the priority he made in his papal ministry of promoting saints and sainthood—all of these things, in significant measure, helped to make Mother into who she was and is.

In these pages we will often call her simply "Mother" because that is what her fellow Missionaries of Charity sisters and those who knew her best, including people on the streets of Calcutta, most often called her. She often signed her letters with that single word and often referred to herself in the third person that way. For all these reasons, although she is now more formally St. Teresa of Calcutta, to many in the world she will always be simply Mother Teresa, or Mother.

There is another important thing to mention here before we get started. Despite all the evidence we had in front of us while she was alive, it is safe to conclude that, nearly a decade after her official canonization and a quarter century after her death, her reputation is still being sorted out. We are learning new things all the time. That is another reason for this new book introducing her life.

Hundreds of millions of people could have articulated Mother Teresa's work while she was alive. They knew she worked among the poorest of the poor in the slums of Calcutta. Those same hundreds of millions witnessed via the media, in her last decade, her famous friendship with the other most popular woman in the world at that time, Great Britain's Princess Diana of Wales. Together, the two embraced needy children. And those same millions saw Mother beside Pope John Paul II, the longest serving and most influential Roman pontiff on the world stage in the twentieth century.

She herself first appeared on the international stage in 1969, when the popular English journalist, presenter, and recent convert to Christianity Malcolm Muggeridge took a film crew to interview her. He became Mother's most ardent early supporter. As if to put a stop to any enterprise such as the book you are holding, he wrote, "The wholly dedicated like Mother Teresa do not have biographies. Biographically speaking, nothing happens to them. To live for, and in, others, as she and the Sisters of the Missionaries of Charity do, is to eliminate happenings, which are a factor of the ego and the will."[6] The documentary that Muggeridge produced, *Something Beautiful for God*, changed everything for her work in India and then throughout the world. That story is told below, in chapter nine.

But what Muggeridge wrote was either disingenuous or naïve. Her life *was* absolutely eventful. She was often at the center of issues of the day. In fact, she put herself there, and she spent many, many days among the other most powerful people in the world. This is also why we continue to be fascinated by her story. This biography places her life in the context of the troubling world events that surrounded her. You will see her living in a convent in relative comfort during the Bengal famine of 1943. You will see her in Calcutta in the midst of the Marxist student movement of protest in 1967. You will witness her in Beirut during the Lebanese Civil War of 1982. Her life's work became so iconic that she too became an icon, and one of our purposes here is to see her for who she was in the context of extraordinary events throughout the twentieth century.

This book is written for more than the faithful who already admire Mother Teresa's work and life. I hope that they will enjoy it and not find me in any way unfaithful. But I also have written for the religiously unmoored, the questing and the questioning, as well as the former Catholic, who knows that there is "something there" in Mother's life to understand better than we have so far.

Finally, it is also the case that few people knew anything about her personal life. This became particularly poignant and evident after her death, when we learned of her doubts about the existence of God. Most of the biographies were written before her cause for canonization was underway, and so those biographers did not have access to the material we now possess revealing Mother's doubts, serious questions of faith, and spiritual loneliness. We will delve into all of these predicaments frequently in the pages to come, and with a retrospective understanding in chapter thirteen. The revelations that surrounded her as her cause for canonization heated up were, to put it mildly, shocking.

In his late-nineteenth-century novel, *Tess of the d'Urbervilles*, Thomas Hardy offers a couple of sentences that I believe help to frame Mother's life and spiritual experience. Describing the very early morning hours when the title character rose to milk cows, Hardy wrote, "The gray half-tones of daybreak are not the gray half-tones of the day's close, though the degree of their shade may be the same. In the twilight of the morning light seems active, darkness passive; in the twilight of evening it is the darkness which is active and crescent, and the light which is the drowsy reverse."[7]

The spiritual darkness that Mother Teresa experienced was always there; at times, it was "active and crescent." In fact, the environment of her ministry could naturally have incubated the darkness. The postulator of her cause for canonization said as much when he connected the beginning of her time working in the slums with the beginning of her experience of darkness and aridity: "As she started her mission to the poor she was plunged into the dark reality of desolation that those whom she served experience: the feeling that God was no longer present, that He no longer loved her or cared for her."[8] Consistently, however, for all those decades, and visible to all of us who were able to watch, Mother went about trying to be the presence of God in situations where only God's absence might otherwise have been felt.

Chronology

August 26, 1910
    Mother Teresa is born Anjezë Gonxhe Bojaxhiu, in Skopje, then part of the Ottoman Empire (now North Macedonia).

1919   Her father Nikollë, a businessman and political activist, dies. He may have been poisoned.

1922–28   She is fascinated by religious life and dreams of becoming a sister.

September 26, 1928
    Having turned eighteen, leaves home to go to Ireland and join the Sisters of Loreto in Rathfarnham. Never sees her mother again. Soon becomes Sister Teresa.

January 1929
    Arrives in Calcutta, India, for the first time. On January 9, is sent to Darjeeling for her novitiate.

May 25, 1931
    First vows.

May 24, 1937
    At twenty-five, takes her final vows in Darjeeling.

1938–1948

Teaches geography and other subjects at St. Mary's High School, Calcutta. Begins to observe terrible poverty beyond the school walls.

August 16–19, 1946

Three days of deadly riots in Calcutta between Hindus and Muslims.

September 10, 1946

Receives what she later refers to as a "call within a call": on a train from Calcutta to Darjeeling, she experiences God telling her to leave the convent and school, to go out and meet the poor.

August 15, 1947

A partition in Bengal separates East Pakistan (which would become in 1970 the sovereign nation of Bangladesh) from West Bengal, still part of India.

August 8, 1948

Receives permission from the Vatican's Sacred Congregation for Religious and from Pope Pius XII to leave Loreto for the slums.

Late 1949 Her dark night experiences, of feeling without God, begin.

October 7, 1950

Receives Vatican approval to create a new religious congregation, the Missionaries of Charity (MC), including approval of the *Constitutions* [or, Rule] *of the Missionaries of Charity*, written by Mother Teresa and Fr. Celeste Van Exem.

1952   Establishes Nirmal Hriday, the first MC house in Calcutta to care for the dying.

1960   Opens the first three MC houses outside Calcutta, in Ranchi, Delhi, and Jhansi.

1963   Founds the Missionaries of Charity Brothers. Brother Andrew joins the order three years later as "General Servant."

July 1965   With the blessing of Pope Paul VI, the first MC foundation is established outside India—in Cocorote, Venezuela, 285 kilometers west of Caracas. The next would be in Rome.

1969   Malcolm Muggeridge television documentary *Something Beautiful for God* begins to make her known throughout the world.

1971   First foundation in the United States, in the South Bronx. Muggeridge's book *Something Beautiful for God* published in the United States. Presented the John F. Kennedy International Award by Senator Edward Kennedy, in Washington, DC, in September.

1979   Second and third convents opened in the United States.

December 10, 1979
        Awarded the Nobel Peace Prize.

1983   Suffers a heart attack while in Rome.

February 3, 1986
        Receives Pope John Paul II in Calcutta.

June–July 1986
>   Tours the United States.

1989
>   In September, suffers another heart attack and is given a temporary pacemaker. On December 1, has a more permanent pacemaker implanted in her chest.

April 1990 April
>   John Paul II accepts her resignation as leader of the MC.

1991–1993
>   More irregular heartbeats lead to two rounds of angiography and angioplasty, the first in the United States, the second in Calcutta.

1992
>   Receives first visit from Princess Diana of England in February, in Rome. Communism falls in Albania, and the MC quickly establish a presence in the nation.

1996
>   Falls and breaks her collarbone in April. Then breaks her foot. Then, at 86, has open heart surgery a third time, in Calcutta, to remove two artery blockages. In November, made an honorary citizen of Rome.

March 13, 1997
>   Sister Mary Nirmala Joshi elected in general chapter to succeed her as Superior General.

September 5, 1997
>   Dies in Calcutta while experiencing her fourth heart attack.

1999   In the case of Mother Teresa, Pope John Paul II extraordinarily waives the requirement that a canonization process may not begin until five years after the subject's death.

October 19, 2003
        Beatified in St. Peter's Square by John Paul II.

September 4, 2016
        Pope Francis formally declares her St. Teresa of Calcutta. Mother Teresa Beatification Day remains an annual public holiday in Albania.

PART I

PREPARATION

CHAPTER ONE

Growing Up in Albania

"She comes from peasant stock and from a community of hill people."
—Fr. Julien Henry[1]

We have photographs of her at school: playing a part in a Christmas play, talking with siblings and friends, and graduating from high school. She seems to have, in the most important respects, led a happy childhood. But like many people who go on to become saints, she learned early of her calling. She was twelve when she first committed to religious life.

She was born Anjezë Gonxhe Bojaxhiu (pronounced *ahn-YEZ GON-ja boy-a-jee-YOU*) on August 26, 1910, in Skopje, now the capital city of the Republic of North Macedonia, a country on Eastern Europe's Balkan Peninsula that was then part of the Ottoman Empire and a half-century later part of the nation of Yugoslavia. This region lies latitudinally immediately above Greece, a country that geographically straddles Eastern and Western Europe, and longitudinally directly east across the Adriatic Sea, the giant body of water that separates the Italian Peninsula from the Balkans.

The identity of Skopje in 1910 was entirely Albanian, despite Albania having long been a crossroads geographically, ethnically, linguistically, politically, and religiously. This is expressed best in one of the standard histories of the place and its people: "For centuries in ancient times, it formed the political, military and cultural border between East and West, i.e., between the Roman Empire of the western Mediterranean including much of the northern Balkans, and the Greek Empire of the eastern Mediterranean including the southern Balkans. In the Middle Ages, Albania was once again a buffer zone, this time between Catholic Italy and the Byzantine Greek Empire. Later, after its definitive conquest by the Ottoman Empire in the fifteenth century, it formed a bridgehead between Christian Europe and the Islamic Orient."[2]

The Italian cities of Bari and Brindisi, at the southern end of the Italian Peninsula, lie only thirty-nine nautical miles from Albania, across the Strait of Otranto. In winter, an Italian standing in Salento (the region that forms the "heel" of the Italian "boot") can easily see the beautiful peaks of Albania's Ceraunian Mountains, overlooking the Strait of Otranto where it flows into the Ionian Sea. *Ceraunian* is Greek, meaning "thunder-split," and some of those breathtaking peaks reach 6,500 feet and more.

Anjezë Gonxhe Bojaxhiu grew up speaking Albanian and was known to family and friends by her middle name. She was, according to her brother Lazar, "plump" and "too serious."[3]

Lazar is Albanian for Lazarus, the friend of Jesus whom the Lord restored to life. His sister was named for the early Christian martyr, St. Agnes. Gonxhe's mother, Roza, was devout and occupied herself both with personal pieties and activities of faith on behalf of others, for example, urging the praying of rosaries in the family and taking in needy children of the community. Her father, Nikollë, was a prosperous contractor who traveled widely for business and was also respected by the priests in Skopje.

Religion on the Balkan Peninsula has always had a nationalist component, often leading to war, and while Roza was a truly devout Catholic, it is probably more accurate to speak of Nikollë as a devout Albanian. Croatia was predominantly Catholic; Serbia was Christian Orthodox; and Albania overwhelmingly Muslim. It is interesting and suggestive that Gonxhe grew up in a minority community of faith. In one respect, to be Catholic in Skopje in 1920 was not unlike being a Catholic in Rome or Athens in the first three centuries of the Common Era. She knew what it was like to be a religious outsider and was therefore prepared for the same experience, years later, when she arrived in Calcutta. She also knew what it was like to practice a faith earnestly and anxiously with a desire that it might continue to thrive in that place. Being Christian in an environment where that identity is far from presumed and is occasionally even challenged tends to help produce disciples worthy of the name.

In other respects, to be a Bojaxhiu in Skopje in 1910 was to be born into an enclave fiercely proud of being both Albanian and Catholic. Albanian Catholics were members of a local church that dates from the fourth century, in lands to which, in the first century, St. Paul himself traveled. St. Paul mentions the Illyrian Peninsula more than once in his writings—see Romans 15:19 and Titus 3:12—and in 2 Timothy 4:10 we learn that he dispatched his disciple Titus to Dalmatia, a region that runs along present-day Albania's northern border. Long before Gonxhe's birth, Albanians had produced cardinals and as many as four popes. Pope St. Eleutherius (c. 174–189), Pope St. Caius (283–296), and

Pope John IV (640–642) are all claimed by Albanians as their own—although at least one of them was probably Croatian. One pope of modern times is also Albanian: to see the portrait of Giovanni Francesco Albani, born in Italy of Albanian parents, who became Pope Clement XI in 1700 and ruled for twenty-one years, is to recognize the familiar features of one of Mother Teresa's kin. Even the great emperor Constantine I, who was the first to make Christianity legal throughout the Empire, was Illyrian-born. The Orthodox Church names him a saint, often using the phrase "Equal-to-the-Apostles," although the Roman Catholic Church does not count him in its calendar of the canonized.

As the Ottoman Empire began to fall apart on November 28, 1912, Albania proclaimed its independence from what was a fledgling Serbia. This was part of the First Balkan War, when nationalist movements in Bulgaria, Serbia, Greece, and Montenegro joined together to defeat their Ottoman rulers. This was a violent and chaotic time when previously quiet feelings of nationalism sprung forth, often at the expense of Albanians who "were the main target of what could be described as a continued pogrom that the neighbouring countries launched either on their own or in conjunction with regional partners to either exterminate or forcefully remove them from territories earmarked for annexation."[4] In fact, the situation was so dire when Gonxhe was a toddler that one scholarly observer was able to report following a tour of the area in 1913: "Houses and whole villages reduced to ashes, unarmed and innocent populations massacred *en masse*, incredible acts of violence, pillage and brutality of every kind—such were the means which were employed and are still being employed by the Serbo-Montenegrin soldiery, with a view to the entire transformation of the ethnic character of regions inhabited exclusively by Albanians."[5]

It is remarkable that they were not displaced along with hundreds of thousands of their fellow ethnic Albanians in the decade following independence. But Albanian pride was ripe at that time and celebrated among members of Mother Teresa's own family. Prior to her father Nikollë's death, he was part of an Albanian nationalist movement aimed at adding Kosovo to the new Albania. (In 1998–99, Skopje was the NATO headquarters during the Western coalition-led intervention in Kosovo.)

Gonxhe was only nine years old when Nikollë died under circumstances that remain mysterious to this day. Her brother Lazar believed that their father was murdered, the cause of death being poison. At least one prominent Albanian Catholic scholar agrees, based on the evidence, and writes: "One thing has always been clear. Whoever wanted to get rid of Nikollë made sure that he suffered a painful death. This explains the choice of the strong poison administered for his execution. According to Roza [his wife], he vomited continuously, coughing up white foam before passing away. The foam would continue to come out of his mouth even after he had died. The poison had been so strong . . . that to protect the mourners his corpse was put in a tin coffin."[6] Throughout her life, Mother refused to speak about this or to recall to others her own memories of the event.

The grief of young Gonxhe was compounded further by what happened next. The family's earthly fortunes changed dramatically in the year following her father's death. His business partners took over the firm he had helped to lead, and the family Bojaxhiu was apparently left with nothing. Perhaps there was legal maneuvering that Gonxhe's mother was unaware of. In any case, the thirty-year-old Roza began to work outside the home for the first time out of immediate necessity, embroidering and selling cloth, in addition to now raising three children on her own.

All these experiences as a child helped to shape Mother into the person she became. As Fr. Julien Henry, the Jesuit who was beside her at the very beginning of the formation of the Missionaries of Charity, once summarized: "She comes from peasant stock and from a community of hill people. An Albanian from Yugoslavia, she is tough and a revolutionary. If the structures stand in the way of fulfilling your ideas, change them, destroy them, ignore them—that is what happened in her case."[7]

The youngest of three children, Gonxhe loved to read from an early age and was very smart. Her facility with language would become even clearer later, when she very rapidly learned English while in the novitiate in Ireland, and then Bengali and Hindi in India. When she finished high school, she began to ponder a career as a teacher. She was already writing creatively, including poems, and seeking to have them published.

She grew up in Sacred Heart of Jesus parish, pastored by a Jesuit named Fr. Franjo Jambrenkovic. The church was in the center of town. Mother would later speak warmly of Jambrenkovic's pastoral impact on her early years in Skopje, and it was he who first introduced her to foreign missions, such as those of St. Ignatius of Loyola in the sixteenth century and the Yugoslav Jesuits who had established a ministry in the Calcutta suburbs quite recently, when Gonxhe was just fourteen.[8]

The Sacred Heart of Jesus later became a Catholic cathedral but was destroyed in the devastating 6.1-magnitude Skopje earthquake of 1963. On the spot where the old church stood, a museum dedicated to the life and ministry of Mother Teresa now stands. The cathedral was rebuilt nearby.

But Gonxhe also learned the faith at home. In *Mother Teresa: In the Name of God's Poor*, a 1997 biographical film whose script Mother Teresa initially approved (though she later, with little explanation, withdrew her approval),[9] her character says, "When I was a little girl, in Skopje, mother used to take me to visit the poor. She taught us that it is our responsibility to help the less fortunate. Sometimes we would come to the dinner table and find total strangers sitting down to share our meals. 'Who are these people?' we would ask. She would say, 'Distant kinsmen.' But they were beggars and destitutes that my dear mama had brought in."[10]

Throughout her teenage years, she spent time alone and with her family at the popular pilgrimage site known as the Chapel of the Black Madonna in the village of Letnica (in present-day Kosovo), contemplating a religious vocation. She would have known, as all Albanians knew, that the Black Madonna—a statue, several centuries old, carved out of dark wood—was said to be created in Skopje before it was carried the seventy-some kilometers to Letnica by Albanians seeking to protect it from iconoclastic Ottomans.[11]

According to family lore, her mother was not enamored with the idea of her youngest daughter leaving home to become a nun. And Roza seems to have taken some comfort in the knowledge that the teenage Gonxhe had so many health ailments that she would likely be rejected in the process of the physical evaluations that were common for all who desired to become missionaries.[12]

Nevertheless, when she turned eighteen, Gonxhe applied to the Sisters of the Institute of the Blessed Virgin Mary (IBVM), or Sisters of Loreto, as they were (and are still) commonly known. This religious congregation, based in Ireland, was founded by an early-seventeenth-century Englishwoman named Mary Ward, who was inspired by Ignatian spirituality. In her letter, Gonxhe explained to them that she knew Serbo-Croatian and some French, in addition to her native Albanian, but no English. She wanted to be a missionary to Bengal, and she knew that the Sisters of Loreto's reach extended that far. She soon received a positive response, asking her to travel by train to Paris for an interview at the order's offices there.

CHAPTER TWO

Sisters of Loreto

"Love proves itself by deeds, so how am I to show
my love?"
                                    —St. Therese of Lisieux[1]

As we have said, Mother Teresa was drawn to religious
life from a young age. She apparently told her mother of
her intention to be a nun when she was still a girl. And we
know that her mother was not enamored of the idea. To
demonstrate the innovative holiness of Mother, one of her
first authorized biographers writes, "Until Agnes went away
to become a nun herself she had never even seen one,"[2] but
this may be a bit of hagiographic excess.

Albania in the twentieth century witnessed several waves
of persecution of Catholics at the hands of Communist leaders who murdered members of religious orders in 1945 and
dispersed and expelled them from the country in 1967. This
happened during Mother's adult years. During her childhood, Albanian Catholics were the subject of deadly threats,
most often from the Ottoman-Muslim majority. A Catholic

minority was still visible, however, in these years toward the end of the Ottoman Empire. Several monasteries, dating from the late Middle Ages, were to be found at this time around Skopje. One was the Monastery of St. Andrew, located beside a beautiful lake just east of the city that remains a popular outdoor destination today. The Monastery of St. Nicholas was another striking medieval structure, in the southwestern outskirts of the city. Other churches and monasteries were scattered throughout the land, despite being sacred to only a minority of people living in Albania, some Roman Catholic, some Byzantine Catholic, and some belonging to the various branches of the Orthodox churches.

When she joined the Sisters of Loreto in Ireland in late September 1928, Gonxhe had arrived in a predominantly Catholic country, which must have given her a brief sense of relief. Seven years earlier, in December 1921, British rule in most of Ireland had finally come to an end, and since that time the nation's government, schools, healthcare institutions, and culture had all become more overtly Catholic in identity. Catholic social teaching, as expressed in sermons and articles and lived in the ordinary life of the laity, had been an essential part of the fight for independence. The Eucharistic Congress held in Dublin in 1932 was one of the largest of its kind during the twentieth century. At least a quarter of the population of the country attended the sessions. Five years after that, a new constitution was passed which declared, "The State recognizes the special position of the Holy Catholic Apostolic and Roman Church as the guardian of the Faith professed by the great majority of the citizens." It was as if what Gonxhe's father had wanted for Albania had just become true in her new, but temporary, homeland.

The church in Ireland did not face the anticlericalism that was present in several other Catholic countries in Europe, such as France and Italy. On the other hand, like most of the rest of global Catholicism, the Catholic Church in Ireland was decidedly nonecumenical. In 1948, the Irish bishops refused to join the newly formed World Council of Churches because, as one author subsequently explained, "it made no sense to do so: Jesus had founded but one church."[3]

In September 1928, Gonxhe traveled by train with her mother and sister from Skopje to Zagreb, Croatia. There she bid farewell to the other two women and boarded another train to Paris. Upon her arrival, she was interviewed for suitability to become a novice. Then she was soon on her way to Dublin and Rathfarnham, a beautiful suburb on the south side of the city, where she took up temporary residence at Rathfarnham House, the name of the grand buildings that housed the Sisters of Loreto there. She was in a land full of vowed religious, religious orders, and clergy. She would only remain there for six weeks.

Gonxhe took Teresa as her new religious name, in honor of the French nun who had been canonized three years earlier, a mere three decades after her death: Therese of Lisieux. From the vantage point of history, beyond the lifetimes of both women, the differences between the two women seem clear. The cloistered life of quiet simplicity lived by the sensitive and at times emotionally overwrought Therese of Lisieux seems incongruous with the robust, stoic, and hardy approach to life lived before the eyes of the world that the woman we now know as Mother Teresa inhabited. But in 1928, the Catholic world was utterly captivated by the figure of Therese of Lisieux, and Sister Teresa was, like her, entering a convent, her days of activism still far down the road.

Therese of Lisieux had joined her order as a teenager, too, and quietly wished (to her journal, and to her confessor and abbess) for nothing but to be "the little flower of Jesus." Penning one of the most often quoted comments of any saint of the twentieth century, Therese wrote, "O Jesus, my love

. . . at last, I have found my vocation; my vocation is love."[4] This was the inspiration to young Gonxhe in becoming Teresa.

St. Therese's best-selling and posthumous autobiography, *Story of a Soul*, was compiled from these private writings and published first in French in 1898, the year after its author's death. Over the following decade, it was translated into dozens of languages around the world, becoming an international phenomenon. Why did Gonxhe spell her new name *Teresa*, rather than *Therese*? Simply this: "Her religious name was to be spelled in the Spanish way since Sister M. Therese Breen [another Sister of Loreto] was already a novice in Loreto [Italy]."[5]

Before she died at the young age of twenty-four, Therese of Lisieux wrote, "Love proves itself by deeds, so how am I to show my love? Great deeds are forbidden me. The only way I can prove my love is by scattering flowers and these flowers are every little sacrifice, every glance and word, and the doing of the least actions for love."[6]

Instead of great deeds, which she compared to a kind of materialism (which was rampant in the West then, as now), she saw herself on "the little way" of much simpler faith. In the years when Gonxhe was growing up, this simple approach to holiness appealed to millions of Catholics, evidenced by the best-seller status of *Story of a Soul*, which became—with Thomas Merton's *The Seven Storey Mountain*—one of the two most-read Catholic autobiographies of the twentieth century.

At Rathfarnham, Sister Teresa spent her time mostly learning English. She had an excellent facility with languages, and it came quickly to her. She was also preparing for her move to India, where the Sisters of Loreto had maintained a steady presence since 1841, when they built their first school in Calcutta at the invitation of the Catholic archbishop and the approval of the ruling British Raj. Catholics had been residents in Bengal since the late sixteenth century.

CHAPTER THREE

Saintly Precedents

"That is what I am . . . a tiny bit of pencil with
which he writes what he likes."
                                    —Mother Teresa[1]

The story of Mother Teresa's work in India is sometimes
told as if she rose from the sea near Calcutta and walked
into the slums to care for the destitute. Or as if she invented
the concept of an apostolate of caring for the poorest of the
poor. She traveled a long way—metaphorically as well as
geographically—to get to India, in fact, and she wasn't at
all the first to do such work.

St. Francis of Assisi famously discovered his vocation in
the first decade of the thirteenth century when he kissed a
leper despite the disgust that the man's illness and deformi-
ties caused in Francis. In the years that followed, Francis
and his followers opened leprosaria and cared for the destitute all over Italy and, soon, throughout Europe and beyond. Care for lepers—known, eight hundred years after

Francis, as victims of Hansen's disease—was central to Mother's vocation as well. It turns out that the disease is quite treatable and not the highly contagious plague upon humanity it was once thought to be. However, it remains remarkable, perhaps miraculous, that Mother Teresa did not contract this severe ailment herself, nor did she die from the tuberculosis that afflicted so many of the people she touched through her decades working in crowded slums. (Many scholars believe that Francis of Assisi suffered at times throughout his life from depression, trachoma, and probably Hansen's disease, a combination of which led to his own early death at the age of forty-six.[2])

Testimony from one of the Missionaries of Charity sisters reveals Mother's teaching on this point and the fearless approach she took that was as countercultural in her own day as it was in Francis's:

> When I first went for leprosy work as a postulant, I was afraid of getting the disease. After a week, I went to Mother to tell her that I could see a patch on my forearm. Mother believed me and asked Dr. S. to examine me, and he said there was nothing, not even a spot. Then Mother called me and said, "I am going to change your place of work. I think you are not worthy to serve the lepers." . . . From that day, I prayed to get over my fear of the disease, and whenever there was an opportunity I would go to them.[3]

Then there were people like Albert Schweitzer and Mohandas Gandhi, Mother's contemporaries, who chose to live among the poorest of the poor and to minister directly and personally to them in the decades immediately before Gonxhe became resident in Calcutta. A medical doctor as well as a trained theologian, Schweitzer went to the central African rainforest to a place called Lambaréné in what is today the country of Gabon, where he built a hospital and served the poorest of the poor. He won the Nobel Peace Prize in 1952, as did Mother in 1979, with the judges noting his extraordinary "reverence for life."

Even the manner of Mother's living her vow of poverty resembles Francis of Assisi's life and teachings. She insisted that she and the sisters of the Missionaries of Charity eat the same as the poor eat, wear clothing no better than what the poor wear, and avoid comforts to which the poor lacked access, like electric fans in their rooms or back-up generators for the houses they lived in. She often traveled with her belongings in cardboard boxes rather than suitcases. She explicitly quoted St. Francis when addressing these issues.[4]

Another quality of Mother's life that was similar to that of Francis of Assisi was her uncommon and apostolic attention to the present moment. Those who were around St. Francis eight hundred years ago were surprised that he would not allow the friars responsible for cooking the meals to soak beans for soup the night beforehand. A friar was to live only in and for today, as Jesus had instructed his followers: "Do not worry, saying, 'What will we eat?' . . . Tomorrow will bring worries of its own" (Mt. 6:31, 34). Mother taught her sisters the same. She said in 1984: "Love is for today; programs are for the future. We are for today; when tomorrow will come, we shall see what we can do. Somebody is thirsty for water for today, hungry for food for today. Tomorrow we will not have them if we don't feed them today." She often used the metaphor of a pencil to explain this further, saying she was poised only to do what the moment required of her. Holding a small pencil in her hand, she said, "See, that is what I am, God's pencil. A tiny bit of pencil with which he writes what he likes."[5]

Which returns us to Mahatma Gandhi, Mother's contemporary in India for nearly two decades—she arrived in

January 1929, and he was assassinated in January 1948—
who insisted on living as a poor man in solidarity with the
poorest of his fellow Indians, to the point of possessing
nothing. His autobiography describes his reading the New
Testament while a young law student in London, before he
had connected with his Hinduism. Gandhi states that he
was moved by the teachings of Jesus to consider becoming
a Christian, but what caused him to hesitate was that he
couldn't see Christians living by those teachings in the
modern world. Muriel Lester, a British Christian who was
a student of Gandhi's, would eventually open a center in
East London modeled after his principles, which were ultimately inspired by both his Hinduism and his love for Jesus.
She wrote, "The strength of Kingsley Hall lies in the practice
of the presence of God, as taught by Jesus Christ, and is an
effort towards the Kingdom of God on earth."[6]

Gandhi also famously said, "He who serves the poor
serves God." Mother Teresa used to quote this sentence as
a way to express her understanding of seeing the face of
Christ in the faces of the poor.

There were also, of course, thousands of Christian missionaries before Mother Teresa, including many who sought
more to help the poor than to "save souls." The young Sister Teresa wanted first and foremost to be both kinds of
missionary. She understood her work, in her late teens and
twenties, as fulfilling the "Great Commission" of Jesus, as
Jesus laid it out for his disciples in Matthew 28. Writing to
the folks back home after her first profession of vows in
1931, a young Sister Teresa described herself as "fulfilling
Jesus' commandment: 'Go and teach all nations!' "[7] She
would do this first through teaching children who did not
yet know Christ.

Jesuit priests, who were doing missionary work in Bengal
long before Sister Teresa's arrival, helped guide her work in

those early days. Two of those with whom she worked most closely were Fr. Celeste Van Exem, SJ, and Fr. Julien Henry, SJ. The practices of Ignatian meditation and prayer were familiar to Teresa before she arrived in India: every nun in the Institute of the Blessed Virgin Mary was trained in these practices. And the retreat in Darjeeling to which Mother was headed by train when she had her life-altering experience (see the end of chapter four and beginning of chapter five, below) was conducted by a Jesuit, Fr. Pierre Fallon. "When asked about that retreat at a later date," writes Eileen Egan, "his only comment was that Mother Teresa seemed unusually quiet and withdrawn, as though lost in meditation."[8] Her Archbishop, Ferdinand Perier, was also a Jesuit.

Despite working as a schoolteacher in India, her faith was not of a theological or bookish sort. Instead, Mother's inclination was similar to that of her patron, St. Therese of Lisieux, who said, "I have not the courage to force myself to seek beautiful prayers in books; not knowing which to choose I act as children do who cannot read; I say quite simply to the good God what I want to tell Him, and He always understands me."[9] This is also another way in which Mother resembled Francis of Assisi, who said to his brothers (in words that Mother Teresa would later quote in talks to her sisters), "Read something very simple on prayer . . . not a big theological explanation of prayer, but just something very simple—maybe how Mary prayed, how St. Joseph prayed, how your guardian angel prays."[10]

Mother's sense of charity, too, reflected that of St. Therese, who wrote, "On the day of my conversion Charity entered into my heart and with it a yearning to forget self always; thenceforward I was happy." And this keen sense of charity in the soul was perhaps tempered—but only in the first seventeen years in Calcutta—by Therese's caution not to overdo charity as penance in the way that some scholars have suggested saints like Francis of Assisi had done: "When Charity is deeply rooted in the soul it shows itself exteriorly: there is so gracious a way of refusing what we cannot give, that the refusal pleases as much as the gift."[11]

Even Roman Catholic nuns running a home to serve the poor in Calcutta existed before Mother Teresa began that same sort of work there. The Little Sisters of the Poor, a religious institute for women founded in France in 1839 to care for the unwanted elderly. Having expanded their work to England by 1851 and the United States by 1868, they had established a presence in Calcutta by 1882. The Jesuit Fathers were their early mentors in the province, just as they would mentor the Missionaries of Charity seven decades later. In fact, Mother Teresa lived with the Little Sisters of the Poor for a short time at the start of the foundation of the Missionaries of Charity. The special fourth vow of the Little Sisters of the Poor—in addition to the usual chastity, poverty, and obedience—was hospitality. To this day, inscribed in large letters in English across the façade of their home in Calcutta is the phrase, "Will Protect You Always." The Little Sisters' founder, Jeanne Jugan, was canonized seven years before Mother Teresa, by Pope Benedict XVI.

All of these saintly forerunners were inspirations to Sister Teresa as she pondered her work and calling in India.

PART II

CALL

CHAPTER FOUR

Going to India

"You have not chosen me but I have chosen you."
(John 15:16)

"Let us make our Society Something Beautiful for God."
—Mother Teresa[1]

India was an ancient land and a part of the British Empire when the young nun arrived there in early January 1929. As Mother's friend Eileen Egan brilliantly summarizes: "Descending to Calcutta, Sister Teresa came to a city bearing the inescapable signs of an imperial past, but where great riches coexisted with squalor and destitution of almost incredible proportions."[2]

She was only three days in Calcutta before being sent on to Darjeeling, in West Bengal, where she would spend her two-year novitiate, a period of study and spiritual preparation for first vows of religious life. Already well traveled at such a young age, she began then to put down roots in her new homeland. As an earlier biographer put it, "The eighteen-year-old young woman was not to leave the province of Bengal for thirty-one years."[3] She studied Scripture, theology, the lives of the saints, and the rule of her religious order. She prepared to teach the native people the faith and principles of a life with Christ in the Roman Catholic Church. She had wanted to be a teacher before becoming a nun, and she would be good at it.

Her experience as a novice is probably reflected in what she later says, in the *Constitutions of the Missionaries of Charity*, is the purpose of each sister's novitiate: "Spiritual formation receives first place, but the human, intellectual and affective aspects must be given full attention and coordinated towards the whole person in Christ. Great attention should be given in our formation to the acquiring of attitudes of politeness and courtesy."[4] Acquiring those attitudes were critical, because the novice was learning habits necessary for living well in close community life.

She made those first vows on May 25, 1931, back in Calcutta. Soon afterwards, she began teaching in the girls' schools run by the sisters there. Chief among the schools was St. Mary's of Loreto Entally, located in the heart of Calcutta but behind protective walls. It remains today one of the city's premiere schools. Mother would teach there for seventeen years, eventually becoming the school's principal, or headmistress.

Six years after her novice vows, on May 14, 1937, Sister Teresa took her final vows as a Loreto Sister. This was the point that, by the order's common custom, she became known to all as "Mother," rather than "Sister," Teresa.

This was a tumultuous time in Calcutta and throughout all India. In 1931, Mohandas Gandhi had led his campaign of nonviolent civil disobedience known as the Salt March, when as many as sixty thousand people were arrested. This was followed by Gandhi's journey to London in September of that year to demand independence for his people from Great Britain. It was a long journey to get to that point. Meanwhile, Rabindranath Tagore, the first Nobel Prize-winner in Literature from the East, was busy building educational systems for Indian children and lecturing on nationhood, with hopes of building what hadn't existed in India in many generations.

Over the following years, Gandhi was frequently in prison for nonviolent protests and other actions, and frequently in newspaper headlines as he struggled near death in self-imposed fasts for causes he believed in. A 1932 fast was an attempt to sway the Indian people to remove the stain of untouchability from their ancient caste system. Gandhi wrote to his good friend, the Methodist ministry C. F. Andrews, sounding like a new Moses: "The fast has to be a fast to the finish or untouchability has to go now. It is a tremendous task. I must test the affection of the millions who have flocked to those meetings, I have to wrestle with God Himself."[5] The Sisters of Loreto, in their compound, had little need to pay close attention to these matters, but one can imagine that Sister Teresa was not unmoved by what she must have occasionally heard and seen.

As an Albanian-born nun, she was set apart from her European fellow sisters by the color of her skin and her still-developing facility with English. The latter affected her teaching in the school. Overall, she was happy at Loreto and certainly said so, but the writings published after her death reveal a slightly different story. She had gone into the novitiate with a desire to serve the poor of India but immediately found herself assigned teaching responsibilities at a school for girls from families who were financially secure and even wealthy. One scholar writes, "Sister Teresa realised from the start that she had joined Loreto under false expectations. Contrary to the vision of Mary Ward . . . the order's main charism in India was not serving the poor. Rather, its mission, from the moment they first arrived in Calcutta, was educating the daughters of the middle class and the rich."[6]

Soon after her final vows, Mother began spending Sundays in the slums of the city. Children began accompanying her down the streets and into the alleyways, chatting and asking questions, and some of them invited her into their homes to meet their families.[7] She seems to have taken her role as "Mother" very seriously from the start, even before she became the founder of a new religious order. It was not, to her, simply the name of a fully vowed sister; she wanted to be a mother to those needing a mother's comfort and care. Pope John Paul II would later identify this quality in her, saying, "It is not unusual to call a religious 'mother.' But this name had special intensity for Mother Teresa. . . . Seeing Mother Teresa's manner, attitudes, way of being, helps us understand what it meant to her. . . . It helped her to go to the spiritual root of motherhood."[8]

Toward the end of the period when she was still living in the convent and teaching at the school, in the midst of the Second World War, the people of Bengal experienced a famine unlike anything anyone had seen for decades. Approximately five percent of the population of what is now Bangladesh and the region of India called East India—three million people in total—died between 1943 and 1944 of starvation, malaria, malnutrition, and other diseases that were a direct result of the famine. And the social fabric of life of families and communities was utterly destroyed for tens of millions of others who survived. There are stories even of the Loreto Sisters struggling to find food for themselves during this time and of Mother going out of the compound to search for supplies. It is generally accepted by Indian historians that the causes of this famine were human-made, the result of detrimental British colonial policies enforced throughout the twentieth century an intensified by wartime scarcity and the demand for human and natural resources.

World War II impacted the lives of Sister Teresa and the other Sisters of Loreto in other ways as well, as their convent was requisitioned by the British Army as an army hospital. Suddenly, rooms that had housed students were filled with beds for the wounded. For a time, the nuns had to leave the premises and even Calcutta itself. This exposure to the pain and misery of the outside world, plus the fear and uncertainty it carried, must have had an effect on everyone. This was also a step for Mother Teresa in the direction of leaving the convent for the greater needs of the world. Her actions on behalf of others, and of protecting and shepherding the children during these difficult years, were what ultimately led to her being appointed principal of St. Mary's School, while retaining her teaching responsibilities, in 1944.

Then, on August 16, 1946, the first of four days of rioting by Hindus and Muslims in Calcutta began. Nationalist Hindus and minority Muslims each felt threatened by the impending independence of India from Great Britain. The Muslim League, then India's second largest political party, demanded separate states in both the Muslim-majority regions in the east and west—what would eventually become Bangladesh and Pakistan. But when talks broke down between Hindus and Muslims, some Muslim leaders called for "direct action." What started as relatively simple protests quickly turned into massacres, targeted killings, rape, and many other forms of violence. Still today, August 16, 1946, is known in Indian history as Direct Action Day, or the 1946 Calcutta Killings. It's estimated that as many as ten thousand people died in riots and religiously motivated fighting over a seventy-two-hour period. At least ten times that many were left homeless.

During the violence, Mother Teresa, the other nuns, and their students, remained mostly safe inside the convent. By now, she was headmistress of the school, and, like the stories of the young Buddha who did not see the suffering of the world until one day when he accidentally and suddenly saw it firsthand outside his family's safe compound, with shock and dismay, Mother came face-to-face with the world in need. As she later related to a friend:

> I went out from St. Mary's, Entally. I had three hundred girls in the boarding school and we had nothing to eat. We were not supposed to go out into the streets, but I went anyway. Then I saw the bodies on the streets, stabbed, beaten, lying there in strange positions in their dried blood. We had been behind our safe walls. We knew that there had been rioting. People had been jumping over our walls, first a Hindu, then a Muslim. . . . We took in each one and helped him to escape safely.
>
> When I went out on the street—only then I saw the death that was following them.[9]

The phrase she repeated here is apt: *Only then I saw.*

Perhaps the most powerful film adaptation of her life, *Mother Teresa: In the Name of God's Poor* (1997), directed by Kevin Connor, opens by juxtaposing footage from real 1946 Calcutta Killings with scenes of the actors playing Sister Teresa and her fellow sisters receiving communion. As noted above, Mother approved the script of this film, though, for unknown reasons, she later withdrew her approval. During the immediate aftermath of Direct Action Day, Mother saw more raw and real life on the streets around her than she had seen in all her years teaching school behind the walls.

It was several weeks after this tumult, while on a train from Calcutta to Darjeeling to attend her annual spiritual retreat, that Mother received a revelation from God—what she came to refer to as her "call within a call"—to leave the convent for good and go out to meet the poor where they are. In Connor's film, the sister of Loreto who was Mother's traveling companion on that train journey finds her visiting the untouchables in the third-class carriage and says, almost scoldingly, "Teresa, what on earth are you doing!?"[10]

CHAPTER FIVE

Discovering the Poor

"The poorest of the poor are our brothers and sisters."
—Mother Teresa[1]

We should not be surprised to find the origins of the Missionaries of Charity in a private message from God to Mother Teresa. We also should not dismiss such a detail as an exaggeration of hagiography. Many people, not only saints, experience revelations from God in quiet and introspective moments. This is not extraordinary, or at least it shouldn't be. What is extraordinary is what happened next.

She was on a train to Darjeeling when she heard (the word need not be in quotes) God telling her to give up her life again, to go out into the world, to leave the convent to do God's work. The day was Tuesday, September 10, 1946—less than four weeks after the mayhem of Direct Action Day in Calcutta. As the opening passage of the *Constitutions of the Missionaries of Charity* reads, "Our Society . . . is an answer to the special call of Christ given to Our Foundress,

M. Teresa Bojaxhiu, on the 10th, September 1946, the day known to us as Inspiration Day."[2] The capitalizing of "Our" in "Our Foundress" is odd, but this document in its pre-1991 state, nearly impossible to find even in theological libraries, is also full of typographical errors. It was written on a typewriter, as are all MC documents still, to this day.[3] Mother Teresa quickly came to refer to September 10, 1946, as "Inspiration Day." She had no doubt as to the message she received nor the interpretation of its purpose in her life. She must have felt that she had already been doing God's work before this happened, but now the call and the work would change.

She was thirty-six years old when this revelation came, and these locutions took place interiorly and continued to come to her in a similar manner for seven or eight months.[4] However, she would have to wait before carrying out the message she received. She needed the permission of her superiors in order to change the nature of her vocation, and they were understandably hesitant to grant it. First, Mother took a request to her spiritual director, Fr. Celeste Van Exem, SJ, who in turn informed the Archbishop of Calcutta of her desire to leave Loreto for a new ministry on the streets.

Interestingly, *Mother Teresa: In the Name of God's Poor* depicts Fr. Van Exem defending Sister Teresa's hearing God's voice before the Archbishop and Mother Superior. In this fictional account that was reviewed by Mother late in life, Fr. Van Exem pleads with the other two to go beyond their assumptions and listen more deeply. Responding to their doubts about one of their nuns hearing the voice of God, Van Exem says, "But she makes a compelling argument: She says that in the face of every suffering man, woman, and child in India we can find the face of Jesus Christ. She calls it 'God's distressing disguise.' "

Celeste Van Exem, SJ, would become an important person in Mother Teresa's life and in the development of the Missionaries of Charity. Born in Belgium, he graduated from the faculty of theology of the Catholic University of Louvain before coming to India a decade after Mother. Two years her elder he became her spiritual director upon his arrival. Van Exem was the first to insist on a period of discernment for her before acting on what she heard. As Mother later recalled, "[He] put me off—though he saw that it was from God, still he forbade me to even think about it. Often, very often . . . I asked him to let me speak to His Grace [the archbishop], [but] each time he refused."[5]

Archbishop Ferdinand Perier, also a Jesuit and a Belgian, had come to Calcutta as a missionary way back in 1906 and had been archbishop since 1924. He too insisted on a period of waiting and discernment for at least one year. That year, as it happened, was 1947, the year of India's long-awaited independence, its partition into Hindu-dominated and Muslim-dominated states, and the widespread violence and displacement of peoples that came with it. At the end of this period of waiting, Perier was satisfied, not on the basis of "the extraordinary phenomena that [she] had experienced," according to one expert, "but rather on the depth of her life of prayer, her obedience and zeal."[6] If, after all that had happened around her in Calcutta and after the waiting period, she was still serious in her commitment to leave a safe cloister for work in the streets, it must be real.

Mother Teresa had to decide whether to apply for secularization or exclaustration. Secularization would mean leaving the Sisters of Loreto in order to fulfill God's direction to leave the cloister for a new kind of work. Exclaustration meant remaining bound to the vows she had taken as a religious while changing the means of exercising those vows for a period of time. The latter process was meant and often used as a tool for discernment; the exclaustrated will often return to full claustration, and the period lived outside the normal confines of a religious institute will sometimes lead to discerning that a permanent separation is warranted. Mother was clear that she desired to remain a nun and retain her vows, even if it meant that she would have to "secularize" from Loreto in order to take on similar vows in a renewed vocation. Her "call within a call" had only to do with adding to the vows a new form of solidarity with the poor.

So finally, in January 1948, with Calcutta more destitute and needy than ever, Mother wrote with Archbishop Perier's permission to the Mother General of Loreto in Dublin, requesting to leave the order—in effect, a formal release from her vows to the Sisters of Loreto. In that letter, she articulates her vocation with language that would soon become familiar: "God wants me to give myself completely to Him in absolute poverty, to identify myself with the Indian girls in their lives of self-sacrifice and immolation by tending the poor in the slums, the sick, the dying, the beggars in their dirty holes and the little street children. In a word—to give myself without any reserve to God in the poor of the slums and the streets."[7]

This request was graciously and speedily granted. Then Sister Teresa had only to confirm the same with the Congregation for Religious in Rome and Pope Pius XII. Before the end of February, this request was on its way from Calcutta to Delhi, where the apostolic nuncio (a church diplomat, or envoy) would then send it to the Vatican.

Despite her own willingness to be secularized in order to found the Missionaries of Charity, the permission from the Sacred Congregation for Religious came back to Mother with instructions for exclaustration: there would be one more one-year period of discernment and testing. She would remain fully under her original vows as a Loreto sister but this time directing herself in obedience to Archbishop Perier. So she wrote to him: "I want to thank you for all you have done for me—to help me to follow this new call. . . . Please pray for me that I may have the courage to complete my sacrifice."[8]

All was accomplished in accordance with ecclesiastical law. Mother had received from all parties the formal permission she required to leave the cloister for the slums, just as God had told her to do. Nearly two years had gone by since she first heard the voice on that train. Such a period of time felt too long to Mother—after all, it was Jesus's voice she had heard so clearly, and it was her nature and faithfulness that led her to respond to it so completely and rapidly. But to her superiors, this period of time felt short, particularly since they were convinced of her desire to do good and seek holiness, so they did not want to steer her wrongly.

Now they had to find the most tactful way of informing Mother's fellow Loreto Sisters of her change of life. On August 8, 1948, the community was informed. It did not go well at first. While Mother was excited beyond imagining, her sisters were worried, even sick. Kathryn Spink tells us: "When . . . the decree was made public, Mother Ita, the superior, took to her bed for a week. Mother Cenacle wept inconsolably at the loss of her invaluable helper and the prospect of carrying the burden of the Bengali school alone in her advancing years."[9]

She had loved the Loreto convent. Despite the determination she showed to leave it (this quality was characteristic of every turn in her life, when she felt she knew the will of God), it was extremely difficult for her to do so. She later told one of the priests who worked closely beside her, "To leave Loreto was my greatest sacrifice, the most difficult thing I have ever done. It was much more difficult than to leave my family and country to enter religious life. Loreto meant everything to me."[10]

But now she began to pursue headlong a new ministry for the sick and dying. Before she moved to the poorer side of Calcutta, she put on a traditional white sari—the kind worn in India by women after their husbands have died—of simple cotton. This was in August 1948. She then took an approximately ten-hour train ride to Patna, six hundred kilometers to the northwest. Patna was then, as now, a major Indian city on the Ganges, with a population in the millions. This was no spiritual retreat. Mother approached the Medical Mission Sisters, who were trained physicians and nurses working in Holy Family Hospital of Patna, if she might come and stay with them for a few months to learn from them. They knew obstetrics. They were trained in nutrition and gastroenterology. They had just begun their hospital work four months earlier. As one of Mother's biographers explains it, "Teresa arrived in Patna with strong ideas about the need for austerity to reinforce the spirituality of her future life and very concerned with the hours of prayers, penance and fasting; the Medical Mission sisters taught her much of practical use."[11]

Dr. Elise Wynen, a Medical Mission Sister who was also for a time medical director of the hospital, remembered Mother's time there:

> We were much too busy to hold long discussions with [her]. She was just fitted into a cubicle, given a chair in the dining room and community room, and included in our day. Whenever there was a new admission, an emergency or an operation or delivery, Mother Teresa was called at the same time as the nurse called the doctor. She would come flying across the lawn and stay with the patient. . . . In that way,

she became acquainted with fatal accidents, mothers dying on the delivery room table, children sick from being abandoned by hopelessly torn and desperate families. She also attended cholera and smallpox patients. As I remember, nothing ever fazed her.[12]

For about a month, Mother Teresa learned from the Medical Mission Sisters how to care for the sick. She encountered illness and death on a scale that she had never before imagined—that most of us could never imagine. The nutritional advice that the Medical Mission Sisters taught their patients proved essential for Mother, too. For example, she had intended that one of the ways that she and the sisters who would eventually join her in this new form of religious life her would live in solidarity with the poorest of the poor in the way they ate. "We shall eat [only] rice and salt," she told Mother Dengel, the superior of the Medical Missionary Sisters in Patna. But Mother Dengel responded, "If you make your sisters do that, you will commit a serious sin. Within a short time those young girls will fall a prey to tuberculosis and die. How do you want your sisters to work, if their bodies receive no sustenance?" Reporting this conversation, her biographer Edward Le Joly adds: "[She] accepted this expert advice. She could not tempt God, could not ask his divine providence to go continually against the laws of nature he had established, and work a continual miracle for the health of her sisters, when food was available. Humbly she changed her plans."[13]

During her time at Holy Family Hospital, she soaked in knowledge, learned to overcome squeamishness, and was introduced to every sort of physical desperation to be encountered in the hospital and on the street. Meanwhile, as she made her way around Patna, Mother began to face vocal critics in the neighborhood who accused her of trying to confuse them with her dress and caring manner for their people. Some of these critics—the devout Hindus of Patna— were certain that Mother was there to convert them and their children to Catholicism. A country of impressive religious diversity, many states in India—including Patna—had passed, during the British colonial period, anticonversion laws that outlawed attempts to convert someone by force or "allurement." Even today Christians are sometimes accused of violating these statutes. For instance, in 2017, a Carmelite nun was arrested and held briefly in Madhya Pradesh, a state in India's geographic middle.[14]

Figuring all this out, Mother faced the temptation of returning to the comfort and familiarity of the Loreto convent. She had a lot to learn and to process. After just under a month in Patna, she would return to Calcutta. A few months later, she recorded in her diary:

> Today, I learned a good lesson. The poverty of the poor must be so hard for them. While looking for a home I walked and walked till my arms and legs ached. I thought how much they must ache in body and soul, looking for a home, food and health. Then, the comfort of Loreto came to tempt me. "You have only to say the word and all that will be yours again," the Tempter kept on saying. . . . Of free choice, my God, and out of love for you, I desire to remain and do whatever be your Holy will in my regard. I did not let a single tear come.[15]

CHAPTER SIX

Missionaries of Charity

"We are really contemplatives in the heart of the world."
                                        —Mother Teresa[1]

She began to plan. A year earlier, as she had begun to dream of the future, she was already calling her new ministry the Sisters of Charity. There is an informality to it that fits her basic humility and desire to be little, as St. Therese of Lisieux taught. What better name could they give to this than Sisters, or Missionaries, of Charity?

Eighteen months earlier, in a long letter to Archbishop Perier, Mother had explained her calling in detail: "One day at Holy Com. [Communion] I heard the same voice very distinctly—*'I want Indian nuns, victims of My love, who would be Mary & Martha, who would be so very united to Me as to radiate My love on souls.'*"

She goes on at some length describing Jesus' words to her about her relationship with him, the nature of the order to be formed, and the kind of sisters it must include. Then she turns to planning and practical details, saying, "Now the whole thing stands clear before my eyes as follows— . . . In the order girls of any nationality should be taken—but they must become Indian-minded—dress in simple clothes. A long white long-sleeved habit, light blue sari, and a white veil, sandals—no stockings—a crucifix—girdle and rosary."[2]

She continues that the sisters should all gain knowledge and experience in the "interior life," so that they will radiate God's love and that they should become also "victims" of God's love, as God asked of her, which can only happen if they remain very, very poor, and offer "no words," as she puts it.[3]

In the years that followed, she would hold fast to the importance of the interior life and teach it to her fellow sisters. In fact, she often made comments that reveal the private, ascetic understanding she had of being a contemplative in the world. For her, this combination of inner life and in-the-world activism was a continual communication and identification with the person of Jesus Christ. For example, an Indian civil servant interviewer once asked her, "With all this difficult work, how do you still manage a sense of humour?" Mother's response is telling in what she does and does not say. She makes no reference to any humor in her life, but only to the happiness and joy that come with knowing she is with God in Jesus as she lives it: "The work is very, very beautiful, you know. We have no reason to be unhappy. We are doing it with Jesus, for Jesus, to Jesus. We are really contemplatives in the heart of the world. Jesus said, whatever you do to the least of my brethren, you do to me."[4]

Even more pointedly, she used to say that Missionaries of Charity were not like social workers in communities because they were also contemplatives. Why was this distinction important? Because, she said, in their hands-on work among the poor and with the needy, "We are touching the body of Christ twenty-four hours!"[5] A Missionary of Charity ought to be joyful, remembering that her calling and her work was divinely inspired and commanded. There was no room for not feeling up to the task. A sister who struggled with depression would not last long in the MC. "Moodiness is sickness,"[6] Mother used to say, referring perhaps to the ailment that the Desert Fathers and Mothers called *acedia*, a term that referred to listlessness, fear, uncertainty. There was, and is, no room in the MC for those who experience it with frequency. But *acedia* may be battled with the deeply imaginative and daily spiritual practices of a MC. This is why would-be sisters, from the start, spent their entire first year learning to be contemplatives. Only a contemplative could, day after day, see the world through the lens that Mother Teresa intended her to.

For his part, Archbishop Perier offered blessings on Mother's plans, but he also did not expect the new venture to last very long. He told a biographer, "In my mind, I gave her a year. When her own Mother General agreed, I decided to send on her request to the nuncio in Delhi. If she attempted such a work and came back to her congregation after a year, nothing would be lost. If the hand of God was in the work, then it would go on."[7]

What a time it was to start something new in India! A country that had prided itself on holding together a profound religious diversity was suddenly and violently split along religious lines. At midnight of August 15, 1947—just one year after the murderous Direct Action Day riots—a formal "Partition" of the Indian nation took effect. Two Indian provinces—Pubjab on the western side of central India and Bengal on the eastern side, the two separated by a thousand miles of Indian territory—became the new nation of Pakistan. (The eastern side would, in 1971, become Bangladesh.)

Gandhi had absolutely opposed this move, and his protests were part of what led to his assassination in January of the following year at the hands of Hindu nationalists. The loss of life in the months following the Partition, as a result of refugee crises and violence, has been estimated at somewhere between five hundred thousand and two million souls.

Archbishop Perier's initial expectation of a one-year attempt by Mother was reflected in the permission he granted her. She would remain a Loreto nun living outside the convent, the indult read, "for one year or less if a shorter period is sufficient."[8]

With Calcutta so close to what was now the eastern border of India, the Partition resulted in Calcutta's rapid economic decline. The US government, which had operated a military base at Calcutta airport since 1942, had left after the Second World War, taking a lot of economic activity with it. The Partition meant Calcutta lost more industry and massive employment fell upon the region. The political situation came quickly to a crisis, and extremists soon took over. All of this led to more poor people in the streets, declining healthcare, and the absence of social services. A strategically located stopover hub for routes from Europe and North America to southeast Asia and Australia, the Calcutta airport remained busy for many years, but when India and Pakistan went to war in the 1970s, it came to be regarded as unsafe and lost its international status. Even Boeing's invention in 1970 of the 747 played a role, reducing the need for stopover hubs and frequent refueling. All of these factors, along with Mother Teresa's rising fame, contributed to establishing Calcutta as a perpetually and tragically poor city in the eyes of the world.

But Mother's basic disposition did not change. "Good morning, Jesus," she learned to say upon waking each day.[9]

This simple practice—as we will discover later—was not the product of a feeling of spiritual intimacy with God. Rather, she said good morning to Jesus each morning because it was her compass. She was asking to be pointed to her day's work, to the people who would be that day's responsibility, in whom she would see the face of Jesus. It worked.

As she would recount in the *Constitutions* of her new religious congregation, Mother heard the following as the call from God for this new work in India and beyond:

> Our particular mission is to labour at the salvation and sanctification of the poorest of the poor by:—
> - nursing the sick and the dying destitutes
> - gathering and teaching little street children
> - visiting and caring for beggars and their children
> - giving shelter to the abandoned
> - caring for the unwanted, the unloved, and the lonely.
>   and by
> - adoration of Jesus in the Blessed Sacrament.[10]

This is precisely how it appears in the typewritten document that she began in a notebook and which was later edited for presentation by Archbishop Perier in Rome by Fr. Van Exem.

Just before this paragraph, Mother Teresa wrote that the sisters were to take the usual vows of poverty, chastity, and obedience—the traditional "evangelical counsels"—shared by all consecrated religious in every religious order throughout the world. Then she added another, and with emphasis: "Our Aim is to quench the infinite thirst of Jesus Christ for love by the profession of the evangelical counsels and wholehearted free service to the poorest of the poor, according to the teaching and the life of Our Lord in the gospel, revealing in a unique way the Kingdom of God."[11]

Fr. Edward Le Joly, SJ, who knew her well, explains, "This fourth vow that all the Missionaries of Charity take is an essential element of their institute, which can never be dropped or changed without the congregation losing its identity. Mother introduced it and made it binding forever because she knew that several congregations that had initially worked for the poor had gradually become schools for the well-to-do. She did not want this to happen with her Sisters."[12] This was similar to how fervently Francis of Assisi insisted on absolute and real poverty for himself and his brother friars during his lifetime, and the Missionaries of Charity have avoided the battles over this issue that were beset upon the Franciscans almost immediately after St. Francis's death.

Another similarity with St. Francis was the anti-intellectual bent of the Missionaries of Charity. Those who wanted to join their work were instructed to learn to love Jesus in the Eucharist and see Jesus in the faces of the poorest of the poor, and to do this learning in prayer. There was certainly no personal owning of books, and possessing books, even for a time, was generally discouraged as leading to distraction. Simplicity in written communication was also prized above any sort of cleverness. As one former sister remembered: "One day Sister Carmeline [the Sister's superior, in her aspirancy year] passed out sheets of paper. 'I want you to write why you want to be a Missionary of Charity,' she said. 'Not many sentences, no big words. Our life is simple.' "[13]

Cheerfulness and joy were prescribed for every sister. "A joyful sister is like the sunshine of God's love," the *Constitutions* read, "the Hope of eternal happiness, the Flame of burning Love."[14] So was devotion to Mary, who was described as "Our Patroness" (although the *Constitutions* for decades retained a typo in the heading of this portion, reading "Our Patronees"!).[15] The Mother of God was of course the first person, at Calvary, to do what the Missionaries of Charity were now in existence to do: "quench the infinite thirst of Jesus Christ." Mother Teresa often referred to Mary as "the first Missionary of Charity" because "she is the first one to nurse Him, to clothe Him, to feed Him, to look after Him, to take care of Him, to teach Him."[16]

There were also practical applications for each vow. For example, sisters would receive a new religious name and would always prefix it with "Sister," in humility. They would also have their hair cut short. Regarding poverty: "We refrain from demands which the poor would not make as regards food, clothing, medical care, recreational facilities, mode of travel or working equipment." Likewise, "we rejoice when these things are really poor and we take great care of them as the poor know how to."[17]

There apparently was also a concern regarding proper dress. This was easily dispensed with: "One of the aspiring Missionaries of Charity had to be dressed up as a postulant in a plain white sari and short-sleeved habit, another as a novice in a white sari and a habit, the sleeves of which covered the whole arm. Mother Teresa herself posed as a professed Sister with the distinctive blue border to the white sari. Photographs were then taken and submitted to Rome for approval."[18]

* * *

Deciding after a few weeks that her medical training in Patna was complete, Mother Teresa returned to Calcutta and the Motijhil slum, not far from her old convent. There she rented a hut, from which she taught children she had gathered from the streets. And when she wasn't teaching, she began to gather the dying up off the streets, bringing them to another rented hut.

Meanwhile, she and the Jesuit Fathers Van Exem and Henry searched for a larger and more permanent place from which to launch this great mission. First, they found a house on Creek Lane in East Calcutta and at the end of February 1949 Mother moved in, making it a convent. She was alone at the beginning—but in less than three weeks she was joined by her first fellow sister: a Bengali woman named Subhashini Das (not *Subhasini* Das, the anti-British activist and politician who was born in 1915), who had been one of Mother's students at the Entally school. She was soon "Sister Agnes," taking the baptismal name of her mentor, Mother Teresa.

The next Missionaries of Charity sister was also a former pupil. Magdalen Gomes joined Mother and Sister Agnes five weeks after Sister Agnes had come. Gomes was soon "Sister Gertrude." Then there were three.[19]

In fact, all the first women to join Mother came from among her former students. Mother's exclaustration had not caused much rift between her first and second callings, after all. What she would soon reap for God in the slums she had sowed in the hearts and minds of the girls she had taught. Together, they begged for their food and for those in their care, and they continued to teach children.

The conclusion of that first year came quickly, and Archbishop Perier needed little convincing that this was a meaningful and necessary work. So, with Fr. Van Exem's assistance, Mother presented to the Archbishop her *Constitutions* for a proposed new religious congregation, and the Archbishop then presented the same in Rome and before Pope Pius XII.

By October 7, 1950—and with a suitable number totaling twelve—the women were declared for the first time Missionaries of Charity.

The postulants were still in Creek Lane, awaiting a more permanent situation, which was found two years later: a much larger and more centrally located space, on one of central Calcutta's main arteries. This is still the motherhouse of the MC today—54A Acharya J. Chandra (often abbreviated "A. J. C.") Bose Road, Kolkata, 700016.

Keeping with the *Constitutions* written by Mother and Fr. Van Exem, the sisters lived poorly in their eating and in their extremely simply accommodations. As a result, some of the Bengali parents of the sisters were ashamed, rather than proud, of their daughters.[20] It was difficult in those early days to see the nobility of living in such squalor, particularly for people who had known little else in their lives and who wished for better things for their children. It has often been said, correctly, that the "nobility of poverty" is only relevant for those who have never truly known it. Nevertheless, these early Bengali sisters shared very poor circumstances quite similar to their immediate surroundings. They continued to teach the kids in the neighborhood, in addition to caring for the dying and desperate, and they balanced their activism with daily routines of prayer and a weekly day set aside for staying at home.

CHAPTER SEVEN

Nirmal Hriday

"I Thirst."

—quoting Jesus from the cross, these words appear
above the crucifix, behind the altar, in the chapel
of every Missionaries of Charity community

In 1937, Mother Teresa had taken her final vows as a Sister of Loreto. On April 12, 1953, she again took final vows, this time as a Missionary of Charity. This took place in Calcutta's Cathedral of the Most Holy Rosary, alongside many young sisters who took their initial vows at the same time. It was also on this day that Mother succeeded Archbishop Perier as the superior of the MC.[1]

Just a few years before those second final vows, while in the passion and excitement of founding the Missionaries of Charity, Mother began to experience "dark night" feelings of being without God, even ignored and unwanted by God. What an extraordinary disappearance this was, in the life of someone so passionately focused on her Lord. This is how she explained it in 1961 to the Jesuit priest Fr. Joseph Neuner, SJ:

> Now Father—since 49 or 50 this terrible sense of loss—this untold darkness—this loneliness—this continual longing for God—which gives me that pain deep down in my heart.—Darkness is such that I really do not see—neither with my mind nor with my reason. . . . There is no God in me. . . . He does not want me. He is not there.[2]

Meanwhile, the *Constitutions*, in combination with Mother's oral teachings—which would eventually come to be called "Mother's Instructions" within the order—clearly marked the way forward for other sisters who would soon come. Those instructions included that a novice was to pray to see Christ in the Eucharist and also to see him in the faces of the poor. This relates to the quotation leading this chapter. Seeing Christ in the Eucharist and in the faces of the poor are gifts that a sister hopes to receive from God, but they are also accomplished by daily and dedicated practice. Mother consistently emphasized the importance of will power for all Christians and especially for Missionaries of Charity. She taught the sisters: "Ask yourself, why is Jesus thirsting? [Is it because] I am not what I should be and for this Jesus is still thirsting?"[3]

She also said, "When we stop giving we stop loving. . . . It is through love that we encounter God." She told them, "Everything depends on my will. It depends on me, whether I become a saint or a sinner."[4] The *Constitutions* instructed the sisters to ask for and expect no more than what the poorest of the poor have in their daily lives; this was eventually modified slightly, in practice, when the sisters and Mother acknowledged that sisters need to be healthy enough to serve.

Each novice's prayer life was to follow the model that Mother had created for herself, which was itself a reflection of what is practiced by many religious orders: daily Mass attendance, recitation of the Liturgy of the Hours in the morning and evening, praying the Rosary and the Stations of the Cross, and focusing one's attention on Christ with frequent attention to shorter and occasional prayers, as well as the teachings of "Mother's Instructions" that were freely available and often posted in common spaces.

Aspirancy—the initial "getting to know one another" stage for joining the MC, which is initiated by personal application and conjoined by invitation—and then postulancy—an extension to continue that invitation longer—together lasted one year. These were followed by the novitiate, which lasted two more years. At that point, a sister would write a letter to Mother Teresa, asking to be accepted for first vows. In her written responses to these letters, as well as in much of her verbal conversation with her sisters, Mother would often refer to herself and her office in the third person, saying, for instance, "Soon we will go to the chapel and Mother will give you the cross."[5]

After first vows came tertianship, which often lasted longer in the MC than it typically does in other orders. Sisters always lived this period in Rome for one year, then spent several years performing apostolic service—serving the poor in different locales and by various means—before again writing a letter to the superior general, asking permission to make final vows.

Amid all of this holy and ordinary religious activity, Mother's period of dark night experience was well underway. After more than a decade of having feelings of "terrible loss," mentioned earlier, Mother explained to her Jesuit director, Fr. Neuner, in early 1962: "If I ever become a Saint—I will surely be one of 'darkness.' I will continually be absent from Heaven—to light the light of those in darkness on earth."[6]

But here she was, holding a light to those who were trying to follow God in the religious order she founded. Knowing that she was feeling little to no personal consolation from God for years on end, it is possible to read some of the instructions in the *Constitutions* in a different light—this one, for instance: "Our poverty which looks upon Jesus as the only treasure worth having requires more than limiting the use of possessions . . . we wish to be poor in both fact and spirit. . . . We willingly learn to rejoice when we are in want or suffering through poverty."[7]

* * *

The order's work on behalf of the dying evolved over time. Mother grew in her understanding of how to do this most effectively. With more than three million citizens who were poor, even by Calcutta standards, in 1950, the need for care and compassion in the slums, which were everywhere, was tremendous. Social services and hospitals existed throughout the metropolis, but they functioned like ships in the harbor of a great city that is on fire. Only a certain number of people could be helped, and many more, including many who were perhaps beyond helping, had to be turned away. Mother's ministry centered on those turned away elsewhere. She saw in them Christ in his Passion. And in the children left orphaned or abandoned or disabled, she saw the vulnerable infant Christ of the flight into Egypt.

Their first house for the dying in Calcutta came into existence with a struggle. Nirmal Hriday, Mother named it, which is Hindi for "chaste heart" or "immaculate heart." The people of Calcutta quickly took to calling it the House of the Dying. It was situated in the center of a neighborhood called Kalighat, in densely populated South Calcutta, beside a popular temple dedicated to the Hindu goddess Kali.

Mother met with opposition from both Hindus and Muslims in Calcutta, to whom the notion of contact with Catholic missionaries was offensive. There were also critics who didn't like seeing a white woman in a sari. Was she pretending to be Hindu? Were they covertly attempting to convert people? Sister Luke of Nirmal Hriday explained in 1990 to a reporter: "We bless them but we don't try and convert them. At the end they may ask for a Bible or a rosary, not because they've become Christians but because it comforts them. They see the sisters hold these holy items."[8]

From those first days, Mother tried to answer questions and explain their work, but it would take time. As biographer Kathryn Spink explains, "Conversion to Mother Teresa meant 'changing of heart by love.' Conversion by force or bribery was something which she regarded as a shameful thing, and the relinquishing of religion for a plate of rice a terrible humiliation. There were those, however, to whom this was not immediately apparent. Stones were thrown at the Missionaries of Charity as they tried to carry the sick into the dimly lit refuge."[9]

There are also stories from those early days of Indians, devout Hindus, and Hindu priests from nearby temples bringing their complaints to the doors of Nirmal Hriday, only to depart with a very different perspective after witnessing the care being given to their own by the sisters.

Soon after Nirmal Hriday was established, it made sense to care for the adults and the children at different locations. Many of the adult women and men who were brought to Nirmal Hriday were close to death, while many of the children in direst need had a longer future ahead of them. So the first home specifically for children was established in 1955. To it were brought dying children but also severely mentally and physically handicapped children who were not near death, once the issue of neglect was addressed. This also became a de facto orphanage, and while Mother did not continue her work as a schoolteacher, she raised many children and helped prepare them to be ready for life outside her children's home, including attending school.

The first decade of the MC was focused on works of mercy in Calcutta, which would always remain the geographical and spiritual center for the religious order. This was a wise approach, but it was also the approach required by canon law. Spink has explained, "Canon Law forbids the opening of further houses outside the diocese by Institutes less than ten years old and the Archbishop of Calcutta was most emphatic in enforcing this rule."[10] But after the sisters had cared for thousands of people from their home base, requests began to come to open houses in other parts of India. In 1960, they would begin to do so, first in Ranchi, a city of more than a million people in the east; then Delhi, a city of northern India that includes the capital district of New Delhi; and then in Jhansi, a city of a half-million about 420 kilometers south of New Delhi.

For thirty-one years Mother remained in India without leaving the country. She had arrived in Calcutta in 1929 and founded the Missionaries of Charity in 1950. That changed in 1960, when she traveled abroad for the first time to the United States, in response to an invitation to speak at the "international workshop" at the biennial conference of the National Council of Catholic Women. The conference was held that year in Las Vegas, Nevada, of all places (though while the initial Las Vegas Strip of resort hotels and casinos was already established by that time, it did not yet have the reputation as a "city of sin" that it would later attain). The keynote banquet speaker was Helen Hayes, the famous actress and outspoken Catholic, then sixty years old. The two women would later come to know each other personally, and Hayes would make contributions to support Mother's work. In an article about the convention, the Catholic newspaper of the Archdiocese of San Francisco reported somewhat inaccurately, "Sister Teresa, of Calcutta, India, foundress of the Missionaries of Mary . . . described the work of her community among the destitute of India."[11] These clearly were still the nascent days of Mother's work and of public awareness of it.

In November 1964, the thirty-eighth International Eucharistic Congress was held in Bombay, India, at precisely the time that the Missionaries of Charity were opening their first home for the dying in that megacity, now called Mumbai, on the Arabian Sea. Pope Paul VI attended the Congress, and upon his arrival millions of Indians lined the route of his drive from the airport to the Congress location. He travelled in a white Lincoln Continental convertible, donated for this purpose by a wealthy benefactor. At the end of his three-day visit to India, during which time he and Mother Teresa were photographed together, Pope Paul donated the Lincoln to the MC. Mother raffled off the car, raising more than $400,000 in today's value.[12]

The following year, in the summer of 1965, Pope Paul elevated the MC to the canonical status "of pontifical right," formally recognizing it as an institution within the church and responsible to the Holy See in its governance. It was soon after this that the order began extending its reach around the world. With several other sisters, including Sister Mary Nirmala Joshi, who would later succeed Mother Teresa as superior general of the order, Mother flew to

Caracas, Venezuela, and then drove over three hours west to the town of Cocorote, where they established the second foundation of the MC.

The year 1968 brought a flurry of foundations of new MC houses: in Rome, Tanzania, and Australia. Always, these were located in poor neighborhoods. Then, less than six months after the first establishment in Australia came a second in that nation, followed by another in Venezuela, both in the spring of 1970. July 1970 saw the first MC foundation in the Middle East, in Amman, Jordan. The first foundation in England came later that year, in the poor district of Southall, London. The following year would see the first open in the United States, in the Bronx borough of New York City. In a remarkably short amount of time, MC houses had appeared on six continents.

These were not then, and are not now, all "houses for the dying." Their ministries vary from place to place and circumstance to circumstance. For example, the Gaza house, established in 1973, is described in the region as a home for mentally and physically handicapped people and for "adult street cases, poor and abandoned," as well as a home for mentally and physically handicapped children. Meanwhile, the foundation in Palermo, Italy, which began in 1974, creates a camp experience—with all the familiar camp activities—for children ages four to fourteen who are resident there.

When the well-known political commentator William F. Buckley, on his public television program *Firing Line*, asked Mother in 1989 why Missionaries of Charity houses serving the poorest of the poor should be necessary in a country as affluent as the United States, she explained that their US houses, in contrast to India, served those suffering from AIDS/HIV and drug addiction, as well as unwed mothers and the hungry. "We don't have so many people picking up off the streets like we do in India or in Africa, but there are many, many people who are in the streets of Washington or New York or London."[13] At other times, answering similar questions about the presence and ministry of MC houses in wealthy societies, Mother remarked that people die of physical hunger on the streets of Delhi and Addis Ababa every day, while they die of "loneliness and bitterness"— spiritual and emotional hunger—every day in New York, Rome, and London.[14]

CHAPTER EIGHT

Working with Mother Teresa

"The call to be a co-worker is a gift of God. In the Gospel of St. John, Jesus says, 'I have chosen you.' He has chosen each one of you to be a carrier of God's love, an instrument of His peace and compassion."

—Mother Teresa[1]

By the late 1950s, Mother was realizing the need to involve others in new ways on an international scale. In 1963, she established an order for active brothers, known as Missionaries of Charity Brothers. These were men who worked in the beginning under the authority of the same superior general as did the women. This was, of course, Mother Teresa. The order received its own superior in February 1966, when Mother entrusted the role—which came to be known as "general servant"—to the Australian priest Ian Travers-Ball, who left the Jesuits for the Missionaries of Charity Brothers, taking the name Brother Andrew.

He was a humble and giving man, a quiet and vulnerable leader. Sophisticated, well educated, and well spoken, he nevertheless eschewed attention, including all attempts to make him into any sort of guru or great teacher.

Brother Andrew saw his role as simply doing the works of mercy of a Missionary of Charity. He echoed Mother's teachings. For instance, he said, "[Christ] proclaimed: 'I thirst' . . . and the people thought He was thirsty in an ordinary way and they gave Him vinegar straight away: but it was not that He thirsted for—it was our love, our affection, that intimate attachment to Him, and that sharing of His passion. And it is strange that He used such a word. He used 'I thirst' instead of 'Give me your love.'"[2]

While giving a retreat in 1993 in western Australia, he said,

> The Gospel of Jesus is good news for the poor, but it is bad news for the self-assured or the self-sufficient. And that of course is why Jesus ends up crucified. Because the ones who took their stand on their own righteousness, they saw that their ground was cut from under them, and they had to recognize that they too were in need, that they were lacking. . . . The community of Jesus is not the religious establishment of the time: the priests, the scribes, the Pharisees, the doctors of the Law. They are the ones who crucify him. And the community of Jesus, as we see in the Gospel, is given very plain: it is the publicans, the sinners, the tax-collectors, the prostitutes. . . . That's where the Gospel is always in trouble with the world. . . . Because the reality is too embarrassing. The Gospel is always giving a place to the poor, to the little ones. And it's hard to swallow.[3]

Brother Andrew served as general servant of the Missionaries of Charity Brothers from 1966 to 1986. He then retired to his native Australia in the late eighties, devoting himself to missionary teaching. Today he is considered by the order to be a cofounder, so great was his example and influence in shaping it to be what it became. "Although our charism comes clearly from Mother Teresa," the order says, "Brother Andrew gave us a particular appreciation of our own poverty as instruments in God's hands, and the wonderful fact that God uses weak and wounded men like ourselves for his own work."[4] Brother Andrew died in October 2000.

Also in the late 1960s, the interest among the laity in the work of the order was growing exponentially and had to be somehow accommodated. The International Association of Co-Workers of Mother Teresa was soon formed, and Constitutions written to govern the work of people in countries throughout the world. These Constitutions were approved by Pope Paul VI on March 29, 1969.

The first Co-Workers were in Calcutta. They worked beside Mother Teresa and her fellow sisters in serving the poor and the sick. But from the earliest days, people who were sick and dying, and who could not therefore offer physical assistance, served as Co-Workers through the assistance of prayer. Co-Workers were also sometimes involved in service projects and fundraising efforts. In the United States, the first Co-Workers were installed in 1971; Patricia Kump, who had first begun corresponding with Mother a decade earlier, was instrumental in establishing the US chapter and later also edited Mother's international newsletter to Co-Workers.

Beginning in 1984, an organization of "Lay Associates" and "Lay Missionaries of Charity," a "third order" or tertiary group equivalent to those found in other Roman Catholic religious orders, came into being. Members remained committed to their spouses, families, communities, and local parishes while also taking on specific responsibilities and vocation in the charism of the Missionaries of Charity. Many Catholic parishes today have Lay Missionaries of Charity ministries that enlist parishioners to work among the poor, assist nearby Missionaries of Charity when possible, and meet together regularly for companionship and prayer. This is often an anchor spiritual practice for people who seek to live by the example of Jesus.

Taking private vows of chastity (either conjugal chastity or chastity in continence), poverty, obedience, and also making a commitment to serve the needs of the poor in their communities, Lay Associates usually meet with one another in their community monthly or biweekly, have spiritual directors, dress modestly, typically wearing a crucifix on a chain around the neck, and try to pray the daily Liturgy of the Hours. They will sometimes include the abbreviation "LMC" after their names.

The vow of poverty, for Mother Teresa, meant that there would be no active fundraising for the Missionaries of Charity and its related congregations. They would rely on the benevolent giving of those convinced of the importance of the order's mission in the world, but they would not ask for it. This is one area where Co-Workers were instrumental. Mother explained to William F. Buckley in 1989, "We have vowed to God, poverty, chastity, and obedience, like all the congregations have, and beside that, in our society, we take a fourth vow to give wholehearted free service to the poorest of the poor, and we don't have fundraising or anything like that, but we depend completely on Divine Providence like the flowers and the birds and beautiful things in the world that you see."[5]

The 1970s brought the introduction of Contemplative Sisters (1976) and Contemplative Brothers (1979) to support the work of serving the poorest of the poor. The Contemplative

Sisters were cofounded by Mother Teresa and Sister Mary Nirmala Joshi, who had grown up in a Nepalese Hindu family in east India, just south of Kathmandu. Sister Nirmala converted to Catholicism at twenty-three, in 1958, and joined the MC a month later.[6] The Contemplative Sisters' first convent was in the Bronx, only a few blocks north of the original MC house in the South Bronx. These sisters appeared the same as their more active members, but they were rarely seen in public. Their charism was more for prayer, in support of the active work.

Mother's own balance of the contemplative and active had to be modulated amid a continued experience of spiritual darkness. Since the origination of the first order of Missionaries of Charity, she had struggled with loneliness and feelings of God's absence, confiding only to a few of her priest-directors for guidance. But over time, with their help, she came to see the darkness as a sort of blessing. She even admitted to loving it at times, because it was another way of participating in the suffering of Christ, who experienced darkness, for instance, on the Cross itself when he cried out.

However, simply put, it was not easy for a woman of such profound faith to live this way. Mother wrote to Fr. Neuner in 1964: "Pray for me—for the life within me is harder to live. To be in love and yet not to love, to live by faith and yet not to believe. To spend myself and yet be in total darkness."[7]

PART III

LEGACY

CHAPTER NINE

Celebrity

Interviewer: "They also say, whether you like it or not, that you are the world's most powerful woman."

Mother Teresa: "Do they? I wish I was. Then I will bring peace in the world." (laughs)

Interviewer: "You can pick up a telephone and reach a President or a Prime Minister because you speak in the name of peace."

Mother Teresa: "In the name of Christ. Without Him I could do nothing."[1]

Mother Teresa was a woman with a quiet presence but not a quiet personality, and this unnerved some people. It also led directly to her fame and influence.

She intuitively knew how to make the most of that fame to support the causes of her charism. For instance, before leaving a commercial flight, she usually asked the flight attendants to gather from the passengers all unopened food items from their trays and give them to her, explaining that she would deliver them to the nearby poor. Despite the odd and unprecedented request, no one could refuse her.

Finding herself often and easily surrounded by crowds of people anxious to greet her, she handed out Miraculous Medals to nearly everyone who approached her or who in one way or another managed to have a personal moment with her. In this activity, she was carrying out what is understood by many to be the instructions of the Virgin Mary herself, offered first to St. Catherine Laboure in an 1830 apparition.

Mother Teresa had a powerful charisma about her that accompanied a humble demeanor; the combination imbued her with a strong sense of spiritual authority that was perceived far beyond the church and its believers. Fr. Ronald Rolheiser has offered a helpful explanation for how this is possible. Explaining the positive impact of a strong ego in a talk to the Henri Nouwen Society in Toronto several years ago, he said,

> We have a very simplistic notion about ego. In our spiritual language and so on, "ego" is a bad thing. But it isn't. If you're going to accomplish anything in this life, you need a big ego. That doesn't mean being egotistical; that's something different. . . . Mother Teresa, did she have a big ego? The size of the Grand Canyon! Mother Teresa could walk into any room in the world and say, "I'm a very important spiritual figure. I'm a gifted person from God." And she was right. . . . Now she wasn't an egotist because she would also say, "But this is not me. This is God." You see, the rock stars sometimes have big egos because they say, "This is not God, this is me." Part of the struggle with artists is to disidentify from the energy."[2]

But this part of her story really begins with a British media personality and his desire to make good television. In 1969, Malcolm Muggeridge was a sixty-six-year-old journalist best known for his humor, sarcasm, political conservatism, and intellectual doubt. It was these qualities that made his interviews compelling to a wide viewership not disposed to piety or certainty. He did not easily let his subjects—often heads of state—"off the hook." He was also, at that point, a recent convert to Protestant Christianity from agnosticism.

Two years earlier, he had interviewed Mother Teresa briefly and found her to be an interesting subject. He surely also recognized that she made for compelling viewing on the screen. In early 1969, Muggeridge came up with the idea of a television feature about her and her work, to be filmed on location in Calcutta. So, with a crew including director and producer Peter Chafer, whose experience was entirely in series television, Muggeridge flew from England to India. They spent five days in filming.

Only fifty minutes long, *Something Beautiful for God* first aired on BBC2 in the fall of 1969. The documentary had an influence upon those who made it and those who viewed it that was beyond the expectations of everyone involved. Mother's work had been revealed in the West by a reporter of the Associated Press three years earlier, but camera footage of her extraordinary vocation—that was something new. The full-color television broadcast of someone doing in the late twentieth century what hagiographers had portrayed St. Francis of Assisi doing in the Middle Ages was stunning.

By the time it aired, a story was already circulating that the filming had been somehow miraculous. It quickly became more than a simple BBC documentary. It was a major media event, revealing to the world for the first time "Mother Teresa of Calcutta." It was also an event in religious history, revealing a living saint. The accompanying book of the same title appeared two years later.

The documentary and book had a quick and dramatic impact on MC vocations, not unlike the way that Thomas Merton's bestselling 1948 autobiography, *The Seven Storey Mountain*, had led to hundreds of new vocations to US monasteries. Eileen Egan, who traveled with Mother for three decades, has said, "Young women, fired by the compassionate witness of the Missionaries of Charity, poured into the training centers that were set up in various parts of the world."[3] Mother herself later acknowledged the journalist's critical role in the success of her work when, eulogizing Malcolm after his death she wrote, "Malcolm is the one who made our works of love for the poorest of the poor known first. . . . I thank Jesus, and I thank Malcolm."[4]

But comments that Muggeridge made, describing the filming process in miraculous terms, further added to the film's luster in the public imagination. In the book *Something Beautiful for God*, he wrote,

> This Home for the Dying is dimly lit by small windows high up in the walls, and Ken [the photographer] was adamant that filming was quite impossible in there. We had only one small light with us, and to get the place adequately lighted in the time at our disposal was quite impossible. It was decided that, nonetheless, Ken should have a go, but by way of insurance, he took, as well, some film in an outside courtyard where some of the inmates were sitting in the sun. In the processed film, the part taken inside was bathed in a particularly beautiful soft light, whereas the part taken outside was rather dim and confused. . . . I myself am absolutely convinced that the technically unaccountable light is, in fact, the Kindly Light [Cardinal] Newman refers to in his well-known exquisite hymn. . . . I

find it not at all surprising that the luminosity should register on a photographic film. . . . I am personally persuaded that Ken recorded the first authentic photographic miracle.[5]

Muggeridge frequently repeated his claims about the filming miracle and his comments about the "luminosity" of Mother Teresa and her work, both at the time of the film's release and in subsequent years. In 1977, he wrote, "To everyone's amazement, including the cameraman, Ken MacMillan's, and mine, this particular footage came out very well, showing the home for the dying, formerly a temple to the Hindu God Khali, bathed in a soft and very beautiful light. There has been some dispute about this. My own feeling was, and remains, that love carried to the point that Mother Teresa has carried it, has its own luminosity, and that the medieval painters who showed saints with halos, were not so wide of the mark as a twentieth-century mind might suppose."[6]

And in 1988: "When I first set eyes on her . . . I at once realized that I was in the presence of someone of unique quality. This was not due to . . . her shrewdness and quick understanding, though these are very marked; nor even to her manifest piety and true humility and ready laughter. There is a phrase in one of the psalms that always, for me, evokes her presence: 'the beauty of holiness'—that special beauty, amounting to a kind of pervasive luminosity generated by a life dedicated wholly to loving God and His creation."[7]

As Mother Teresa's public persona grew, it became common for people to echo the idea of her personal "luminosity" and "radiance." Did Muggeridge's depiction become a kind of icon that replaced the real person, or was there a reality there that was recognized by many of those who encountered her? It is impossible to say. Or perhaps the awe she inspired manifested itself often in a sense of light. The Hindu photographer Raghu Rai, who came to know Mother well, once described seeing "a tiny creature lit with beatific radiance," calling her "a *Darshan* [an image of a deity or holy person, in Hinduism] of 'His' magnificence," adding, "my camera became inadequate."[8]

Despite these experiences people had of her luminosity, we also know now that Mother often felt the opposite of this. Precisely when *Something Beautiful for God* was reaching millions of people, and Mother's appearances with Muggeridge were most frequent, was the time when the postulator for Mother's cause of canonization tells us: "[She] had reached the point in her life when she no longer ventured to penetrate or question the mystery of her unremitting darkness. She accepted it, as she did everything else that God willed or at least permitted, 'with a big smile.' "[9]

Muggeridge eventually converted to Catholicism in 1982, at age 79. He attributed the step, in large part, to Mother's influence. As his biographer tells it: "He frequently alluded to a conversation he had with Mother Teresa while walking along the Serpentine in London. As they strolled through the park, he explained to her that he shared Simone Weil's belief that God needed Christians outside the Church as well as inside. 'No, he doesn't,' she said to him tartly. There was something about her simple confidence that seemed to him to cut through all his evasions."[10]

In a eulogizing letter written in 1995, five years after his death, Mother spoke again of her admiration: "When I think of Malcolm Muggeridge, I hear again the words 'I THIRST.' Jesus thirsted for Malcolm to know Him as truth and as love. He kept calling Malcolm and year by year drew him closer to Himself. . . . What a joy it was for Jesus and for Malcolm when they were united in the Sacraments of the

Church. Now, I trust, Malcolm's thirst for Jesus and Jesus' thirst for Malcolm are fully satisfied in heaven."[11]

* * *

Skepticism is common among those who read about Mother Teresa's life. Credulity can be a blessing and a gift, but it also can lead to many problems. The Sanskrit word mentioned in the comment by the photographer Raghu Rai above, *darshan*, literally means "to view," but it is used in a spiritual context to refer to glimpsing, or beholding the holiness in a deity or a special person. This concept might be used to explain the power of the presence of a saint like Mother Teresa. A similar idea is found in Christian practice when a blessing comes from just seeing, hearing the voice, or touching the clothes of a holy person. This was expressed countless times by those who were in Mother's presence. This may say something less about her than about the person who feels so moved.

Two years after that famous initial BBC broadcast, Mother and Muggeridge appeared together from New York City on a Sunday morning network television program called *Inquiry*, hosted by Paulist Fr. James Lloyd, on WNBC, Channel 4. Mother was in the city to work on setting up the first Missionaries of Charity convent in the Bronx. It was early October 1971. Muggeridge was promoting his book, *Something Beautiful for God*, which had just been published in New York, half a year after its release in London. Toward the end of the interview, Muggeridge explains why he thinks Mother's message and work is so important in their time: "I feel that it really boils down to the kingdom of heaven on earth. If you consider goodness in terms of the dimensions of time and earthly society, you are inevitably drawn into making these distinctions between human beings: You say, 'Now that man, that's a valuable life. This not a valuable life.' . . . Mother comes along and will not accept those categories at all."[12]

Mother and Muggeridge had many more interviews that day and week, including one with Barbara Walters on NBC's *The Today Show* and another with David Frost on the set of *The David Frost Show*.[13] An ad for the book appeared in *The New York Times*. Her unique combination of celebrity and humility became the key elements of the narrative about her and the first signals of her eventual sainthood. A 1978 press release from John Carroll University in Cleveland, Ohio, where Mother was to receive an honorary doctorate, read: "In India, her normal day begins at 4:30 a.m. Prayer and mass precede breakfast, usually consisting of an egg, bread, banana and tea. The woman, who has spoken with prime ministers and popes, then goes out into the city and tends to its lepers, retarded and poor."[14]

Back in Calcutta, the famous came to her, often for the impact of the visit on their own fame or electability. Senator Edward Kennedy, in the midst of considering a run for the US presidency, visited Mother in 1971. Later that year, in Washington, DC, he presented her with a John F. Kennedy International Award.

The awards and international recognition would continue without abatement for the rest of her life. Indira Gandhi, as she finished her first term as prime minister of India and in her capacity as chancellor of Viswa Bharati University in West Bengal, conferred on Mother a PhD in Literature in 1976. In 1983, Queen Elizabeth of England met Mother in New Delhi to confer upon her the insignia of the highly exclusive honor of the Order of Merit, which may be held by only twenty-four living members at any one time and only eleven of which have ever been conferred on non-British citizens.

This is not to suggest that Mother was impressed by her own celebrity or by the celebrities whom she came to know. After receiving the Noble Prize in Sweden in 1979, she traveled to Rome to visit her sisters there. One of them remembered, "Mother said, 'It's not important, Sisters.' Later, Sister Gertrude told us that whenever Mother received a prize, she never looked at it again. She always left it in the convent where she happened to be, then later the sisters quietly brought the award to Mother House and locked it in a cupboard near Mother's room. Mother sometimes asked what was in the cupboard. The sisters would say, 'Nothing important, Mother,' because that's what Mother always said about awards."[15]

But the combination of extreme humility and great celebrity sometimes intersected in curious ways. When an interviewer commented to her, "You once said to me that the greatest fear a human being can face is the fear of humiliation," Mother replied, "The surest way to be one with God is to accept humiliation." When the interviewer followed up by asking, "Have you encountered humiliation?," Mother replied, "Oh, yes, plenty. This publicity is also humiliation."[16]

Her celebrity also brought some significant criticism. Because Mother did not ask questions of those who made financial donations to her work, the Missionaries of Charity were sometimes unwittingly associated with unsavory people and groups. Her avoidance of taking sides of political issues often felt problematic to other Christians. For example, when Mother wrote, during the buildup to the First Gulf War between the United States and Iraq, an open letter to the leaders of both countries, saying, "You both have your cases to make and your people to care for but first please listen to the One who came into the world to teach us peace," many observers found this to be naïve. Catholic actor and peace activist Martin Sheen has written about his meeting with

Mother in Rome in February 1990, as the war in the Persian Gulf raged. He and fellow activist Joe Cosgrove sought to deliver a brief that Cosgrove, a lawyer, had prepared, asking Pope John Paul II to bring the issue of the war to the World Court. Sheen later wrote,

> We were told she was awaiting our arrival, so we gathered our things and hurried to meet her. We arrived at the nondescript door of a structure that had once been a large chicken coop but which now housed the sisters and Mother Teresa when she was in town. This was a place of utter humility, service and prayer. As we were ushered into a room, we saw a small chapel stacked with clothes that were to be distributed to the poor. In a moment, a tiny figure in a white sari with blue stripes met us with a broad welcoming smile. It was the living saint of Calcutta.
>
> It was immediately clear that to her, no one was a stranger. In an instant, we were her friends, as if we had known one another all our lives. It wasn't a skill, nor an act; it was just who she was.

Sheen continued:

> Joe said that he had written a brief for the Holy Father that explained that the war violated several principles of international law and that a ruling from the World Court could, perhaps, spark a concerted effort to bring it to an end. Mother was patient but not terribly interested in the polemics. She had given Joe the floor, so she just listened, and when he finished she took the brief and matter-of-factly said that, indeed, she would be with the Holy Father in the morning and would deliver it to him in person. In utter humility, she asked: "What else can I do? I've written to the presidents but have not received a reply, so what can I do?"

And then:

> The next day, a few hours after Mother's visit, Pope John
> Paul II held his weekly audience and issued one of his
> strongest rebukes of the war to date. Perhaps something
> had taken root.
>
> Mother had invited us to join her and her community
> for early Mass the next morning. Very early. I met Joe in
> the hotel lobby around 4:30 a.m. and told him what I'd
> heard on the news: There was a rumor that a cease-fire in
> the Gulf was imminent. When we arrived at Mother's cha-
> pel, the news was confirmed: The war was over![17]

But saints are often naïve, and their sanctity can sometimes rely on this. She befriended everyone. She cared for
everyone without distinction. Even in the case of biographers, we find several whose books are declared to be "authorized." Surely Mother Teresa said "yes" most of the time
when someone expressed an interest in her work, which she
knew to be the work of God.

This is not to suggest that she was easy to work with. On
the contrary, saints are often difficult people relationally,
expecting others to bend to accommodate their drive and
vision. For example, Fr. Benedict F. Groeschel, CFR—an
influential and powerful Catholic leader who died in 2014
and could one day himself be a subject for canonization—
once reflected on working with her as an administrator for
the Archdiocese of New York:

> It wasn't a lot of fun dealing with Mother Teresa. . . . She
> was directed by an inner vision and sight which I didn't
> have. . . . Sometimes they were wounds. I can understand
> people being mad at Mother Teresa. But she always did
> things because she thought it was the will of God. Was she
> always right? I doubt it. Nobody is always right. The last

person who was always right, they crucified him. . . .
There's no place in the gospel where Jesus says to the
apostles, "Hey fellas, what do you think? Should we go to
Damascus, or should we go down to Jerusalem?" He said,
"We're going to Jerusalem, period."[18]

Because political figures sought her counsel—and a good
photo opportunity—Mother became a political figure without intending to. Her March 1990 meeting in Calcutta with
Yasser Arafat—the founder and chairman of the Palestinian
Liberation Organization, responsible for extensive guerilla
warfare and terrorism against Israel and its citizens in its
struggle for an independent Palestinian state—prompted
intense criticism. Mother's perspective was always that she
was there to offer Christ's presence to whomever came calling, and the Missionaries of Charity had been a presence in
both Jerusalem and Gaza since the early 1970s.

Diana, Princess of Wales, also came to see Mother, visiting
her in Rome. In February 1992, Diana was undertaking
benevolent causes all over the world, often in front of television cameras. She was also looking for spiritual direction,
perhaps even a new spiritual home. Diana had already sat
at the bedsides of patients suffering from HIV/AIDS and in
1987 famously held the hand of a man suffering from the
still-misunderstood disease, to help remove its stigma. These
gestures of familiarity and outreach were giant steps forward for the British royal family, of which Diana was still
a part, in terms of relating to people. She also had visited
leprosy hospitals in far-reaching places like Indonesia before
she made her way to Mother in Rome and then later at the
Home for the Dying and Destitute in Calcutta.

Diana's extramarital affairs were also public knowledge
by this time. No one knows exactly what she and Mother

discussed for the near-hour they spent together that winter day in Rome, much of it together alone in the chapel. In a note written by hand to her butler and confidante Paul Burrell on the day of her encounter with Mother Teresa, Diana said, "Today something really profound touched my life. I went to Mother Teresa's home and found the direction I've been searching for all these years."[19]

CHAPTER TEN

Living as an Indian, Traveling the World

"There should be less talk; a preaching point is not always a meeting point. What do you do then? Take a broom and clean someone's house. That says enough. All of us are but His instruments who do our little bit and pass by."

—Mother Teresa[1]

Despite her constant attention to Missionaries of Charity work and her disinterest in politics, Mother Teresa nevertheless involved herself often in world events.

Perhaps most important to her was when she was able, in 1992, to watch Communism dissolve in her native Albania and to play an active role in the process. The revolutions that began throughout the Eastern Europe in 1989 occurred in Albania as well, particularly through student-led organizations and protests. By 1991, democratic elections were called in Albania, and the Communist Party retained its majority in the new Parliament. But the following year, the new Democratic Party won in the general election, ushering in a brief period of optimism and a government known as the Fourth Republic. More than four decades of official atheism came to a swift end. (This was followed in 1997, the year of Mother's death, by resignations of key leaders and a brief civil war.)

She had experienced problems and difficulties with governments before. In the early 1980s, she and the MC were refused entry to Nicaragua during the bloody Nicaraguan Revolution, after Mother made statements, common among many institutional leaders within the Catholic Church at that time, supporting the US-backed Contras who were expected to use their power to return the Catholic Church to its privileged position in Nicaraguan society. She had also been thwarted in the late 1980s and early '90s by the government of China in her attempts to open a convent in that nation (following her successful opening of missions in Yugoslavia and East Germany, two other countries not yet tolerating religious "interference" in state matters). But she could politic. When Mother was interviewed by reporters in Hong Kong, after having just spent four days in Peking (known today as Beijing) with Chinese officials, she downplayed the urgency for a mission in mainland China, saying, "According to what I've heard, most of this [charitable work] is taken care of by the government."[2]

In 1988, as the antiapartheid movement was at its passionate peak in South Africa, and after a personal meeting with Cape Town Archbishop Desmond Tutu in Paris, Mother founded the first MC foundation in South Africa in Khayelitsha, in the center of a Black neighborhood. She denied being politically motivated, however, saying that she was simply responding to the invitation of the Catholic archbishop of

Pretoria, George Francis Daniel. Archbishop Daniel was a noted antiapartheid figure in the country, but Mother said, "I did not know that apartheid or something like that existed. I never mix up in politics because I do not know."[3]

The advent of a democratic Albania after the fall of Communism prompted a new wave of the Albanian diaspora to countries such as Italy, Argentina, and Greece, but also renewed efforts to support missionary work in Mother's homeland. Mother had begun to found a MC house in Albania in March 1991, when the democratic rumblings first began. She had prayed, even begged, for this opportunity for decades, often before the Albanian ambassador to Italy on her visits to Rome.[4] In fact, she had first returned to Skopje back in 1980, when the city and the rest of Albania were then part of Yugoslavia, under Soviet control. There wasn't much enthusiasm for her Catholic teachings and values in the Soviet republic, and yet she was declared an honorary citizen of Skopje, and it became common to refer to her in her native land as "Mother Teresa of Skopje."

The public celebration of the MC presence in her homeland took place simultaneously with a papal visit, when John Paul II became the first Roman pontiff of the modern era to visit Albania in late April 1993. At that time, the Balkan nation was known throughout the world as the native land of Mother Teresa.

In one whirlwind day, April 25, Pope John Paul II established four bishops for the country (two would be made cardinals a year later), inaugurated a cathedral in Shkodër (called *Scutari* in Italian and English) in the north, and then met Mother Teresa in Tirana, Albania's capital. In the last of his talks, with the new president of the country by his side, the pope said to an immense crowd at Piazza Scanderbeg di Tirana:

> After an intense day of celebrations and meetings, which gave me the opportunity to touch not only the vibrant faith of the Catholic community, but also the warm hospitality of the Albanian people, the time has come for my farewell and it is with deep emotion that I am about to leave you. In the friendship you showed me, I felt the heartbeat of people capable of profound feelings; in your open frankness I saw the courage of a young democracy definitely set out on the paths of freedom, after long and dark years of dictatorship and suffocating atheism. Thanks for welcoming us! I return to Rome with the vivid memory of your land imprinted on my mind and heart. Thank you![5]

Mother then broke what had been a decade-long gap in granting televised interviews to tape one that would appear on the BBC in May. The presenters introduced her as Albania's "most famous daughter," and she said to interviewer Bill Hamilton, "The people, you can look now on their faces and see that there is really peace. The first time I came here, it was completely different."[6] (She was referring to a previous return to her homeland two years earlier.)

Also in the early 1990s, the first Missionaries of Charity presence in Yemen was created when Mother Teresa convinced the prime minister of this Muslim-majority country, where Christian missionaries and conversion from Islam had been outlawed, to welcome the presence of a house for the dying. The first was established in Aden, a city of nearly a million people that lies near the eastern approach to the Red Sea, in 1992, followed soon by houses in three other Yemeni cities. The order would pay a heavy price when, on March 4, 2016, unknown gunmen attacked the Aden home, killing sixteen people, including four MC sisters. At the funeral a week later, the Patriarch of Jerusalem Fouad Twal presided and said in his homily, "We do not send our condolences, we congratulate you for the gift of their lives and yours, for all that you do to serve the poorest of the poor."[7]

So she was worldly, wise, and savvy. Mother knew how to use her influence to avoid red tape and then how to persist when bureaucracies or government policies stood in the way of her mission. There were dozens of other international journeys, for decades, including many to the United States. She was tireless.

For example, on October 18, 1972, she arrived in Salt Lake City, Utah, an unlikely place for a Catholic luminary. She was picked up at the airport by two monks from Holy Trinity Abbey in Huntsville, Utah, a Trappist community that has since disbanded. "No one noticed them. A large crowd was there hoping to see the Osmonds [a family of singing stars, including the soon-to-be-famous teenage Donnie Osmond, from Utah], who arrived at the same time," according to one account. She had been invited to Utah, and the Trappist community, by one of their monks, Brother Nicholas, who had worked closely with her in Calcutta. Most of her destinations were the result of personal invitations of this sort, without international ramifications or political entanglements.

Meanwhile, back in India, the original work of mercy continued, and Mother became a frequent spokesperson for Catholic teaching worldwide. Although she wasn't interested in interfaith conversation, she was often recognized for ministering among Hindus and Muslims, without aiming to convert them, and there were times when she made comments of an almost surprising openness to non-Christian viewpoints. For instance, she said, "Whether one is a Hindu or a Muslim [the two majority faiths in India] or a Christian, how you live your life is proof that you are or are not fully His. We cannot condemn or judge or pass words that will hurt people. We don't know in what way God is appearing to that soul and what God is drawing that soul to; therefore, who are we to condemn anybody?"[8] The first sentence echoes Catholic social teaching, and the last two sentences are similar to comments made by Pope Francis, decades later, which put him under scrutiny from his more conservative critics.

But as a Catholic religious sister living in an overwhelmingly Hindu country, caring daily for Hindu people, it is notable that she rarely met with their religious leaders, and she showed little interest in the Catholic-Hindu dialogues that were maintained—both in academic contexts and in lived experience "on the ground" in India—by some of her notable contemporaries. These included the British-born Fr. Bede Griffiths, OSB Cam; the Frenchmen Dom Henri Le Saux, OSB (also known as Abhishiktananda) and Abbé Jules Monchanin; and Spanish priest, Raimon Panikkar—all authors of books on the subject of bridging faiths and spiritualities. Mother Teresa was born within a decade of Griffiths, Le Saux, and Panikkar. Monchanin, Le Saux's teacher, was slightly older. In contrast to these fellow Catholics, she focused on action, always, over conversation. As she famously instructed her fellow sisters in 1981, "Don't look for big things, just do small things with great love."[9]

The impact of her work in India was felt, and recognized, across religious divides. As one Catholic interfaith expert explained: "Mother Teresa's funeral was perhaps the best evidence of her vitality as an interfaith symbol. The Indian government, composed primarily of Hindu members, honoured this 'saint of the gutters' with a state funeral, a recognition normally reserved for heads of state. This honour . . . is even more amazing when one considers that Hindus and the Indian government have long been suspicious of Christian missionary work in India."[10]

This is most often the way of saints, focusing on what needs doing. Like others before and after her, she also often seemed impatient with talk altogether. One Hindu man who knew her well remembered an elderly Brahmin (the spiritually elite class of traditional Hinduism) woman who had been dying on the streets when some Missionaries of Charity wanted to help her. The devout woman, despite her desperate condition, refused to allow them to move her, saying she could only be touched by another Brahmin. When Mother Teresa was informed, she went out to see the woman personally. When the woman asked Mother if she was a Brahmin, Mother replied, "Yes," and carried her inside.[11] Indeed, there were other occasions when she claimed the title of Brahmin for herself in order to expedite the care of someone in need. She said, "For the Hindus, a Brahmin is a holy person because they are consecrated to God. . . . I could say I am a Brahmin because I really belong to God."[12]

There is an essential Jewish teaching called *Pikuach Nefesh*—"saving a life"—an obligation or mitzvot that says saving a human life takes priority over everything else, even if and when it means breaking another commandment in the Torah. Perhaps Mother Teresa had something like this in mind when she lied to the dying woman. It was the work of mercy, the extending of love through personal action, that mattered most to her.

At other times, she met criticism head-on, but even in her words showed the primacy of action. We have this account from her talk to an audience of monks in 1972:

> Mother Teresa told how her Calcutta house for the dying was in a temple formerly dedicated to a Hindu goddess. Many Hindus objected to her presence there and protested, shouting, "Kill Mother Teresa!" The loud demonstrators

disturbed her patients, so she confronted them, saying, "You want to kill me? Kill me! I'll go to Heaven, but you must stop this nonsense!"

They stopped it. Later, the protesters brought her a Hindu priest stricken with tuberculosis. No other hospital would take him in. Mother Teresa did, and she personally cared for him until he died peacefully in the former temple.[13]

CHAPTER ELEVEN

Facing Critics

"Why did they do it?"

—Mother Teresa, after a program criticizing
her work aired on British television[1]

Saints aren't always nice, and they aren't always gentle. Those who knew Mother Teresa personally knew she could show a quick temper. One of her own authorized biographers, a writer who clearly admired her subject, wrote in the preface of her book about Mother, "She was, I discovered, not only humble and small but also strong-willed, resolute, determined and totally fearless, because God was on her side."[2] These are not the qualities of a typical collaborator or colleague. Neither are they qualities of a "nice" person. She was accustomed to being in charge.

Indian photographer Raghu Rai, who first met her in the early 1970s and produced several books of glowing appreciation for her work, remembered the day they first met (writing as if he were addressing Mother Teresa directly):

I was young, in my late twenties, and always eager to do something different. . . . [While you were talking with my editor,] I caught a glimpse of three sisters who were standing on the first floor with prayer books in their hands. They were visible only with the flickering movement of the half curtain behind you. This was a compelling moment. Instinctively, I started taking pictures.

"What the hell on earth are you doing there?" you thundered. I was taken aback. "Mother, there are three sisters praying and they look like angels," I said, all excited. How you melted, Mother, and accepted that moment.[3]

But the same author depicts her as a woman who is able to empathize and change, a woman without rigidity. Rai recalls that during an early experience photographing Mother Teresa and her Missionaries of Charity in their motherhouse in Calcutta, she instructed him not to capture them at prayer, saying that such moments should remain personal, and private, not for public consumption. He quietly objected and pleaded with her to change her mind. Writing again as if he's speaking to her, he remembers, "You agreed on this condition: 'You will sit in one place to take pictures.'" But, as the moment comes, the photographer is caught up in it and begins to move about the room, snapping pictures. He recounts what happened next:

I moved toward you, with the burden of my guilt and implored your forgiveness with my eyes for having failed to keep my word. "Mother, I am sorry, I could not remain in one place as you had asked me. Please forgive me," I said.

You took my hands into yours, looked deep into me and said, "God has given you this assignment. You must do it well." Mother, how I thanked you for forgiving me.[4]

It turns out that Mother Teresa had many critics, particularly in the last decade of her life. One thing that many people questioned was her tactics. No one can criticize caring for and feeding children who has been consigned to life in the gutters, but what about standing up and shouting, "Why are these children in the gutter!?"

She summarized her own life's work with an example in her Nobel Prize acceptance speech:

> I never forget when I brought a man from the street. He was covered with maggots; his face was the only place that was clean. And yet that man, when we brought him to our home for the dying, he said just one sentence: I have lived like an animal in the street, but I am going to die like an angel, love and care, and he died beautifully. He went home to God, for dead is nothing but going home to God. And he having enjoyed that love, that being wanted, that being loved, that being somebody to somebody at the last moment, brought that joy in his life.[5]

But is it enough to simply provide the destitute with an honorable end to a miserable life?

She was aware of these criticisms for decades—a critique that people have leveled against many other saints over the centuries who were dedicated to works of mercy and who did so from a position of a vow of poverty. She moved quickly and did not worry much about tomorrow. She responded to the needs of each day. She said, "We do not make plans. We do not prepare infrastructure."[6]

There were also those who questioned her associations with certain benefactors, since she famously never refused a donation from someone who wanted to support the order's work. Chief among the questionable donors was the newspaper titan, Robert Maxwell, described in one newspaper op-ed as a "corporate kleptomaniac, ruthless bully and possible war criminal."[7] These were allegations based on evidence, but Mother Teresa did not seem to pause to consider them carefully before accepting Maxwell's money to fund her activities in the late 1980s. Similar charges of bad associations were levied for her 1981 visit to Haiti to accept an award from Haiti's then-dictator, Jean-Claude Duvalier. Why would she accept such an invitation? She believed in her missionary activities first and foremost. Another questionable association was with Catholic fundamentalist Charles Keating, who, like Maxwell, was involved in illegal, exploitive, and immoral financial activities, and yet Mother accepted his millions, as well, to support the works of charity.

Contrary examples from her life abound. For example, legendary actor and radio broadcaster Pat McMahon remembers vividly the day he interviewed Mother Teresa in 1989, when she was in Phoenix, Arizona, to open a new homeless shelter in the city. McMahon had her on his radio show and asked her, "Can I help you raise money for your mission? What would you like to tell our listeners?" Her response was simply, "Tomorrow morning get up and go out onto the streets in Phoenix. Find someone who believes that he is alone, and convince him that he is not."[8]

She has had other critics, including the noted British columnist and author Christopher Hitchens. A self-styled "devil's advocate," Hitchens published a scathing, provocative critique of Mother, in a 1994 British television documentary called "Hell's Angel" and then a year later in a book called *The Missionary Position.* He detailed the Maxwell, Duvalier, and Keating relationships and was troubled by other aspects of her life. A *New York Times* critic summarized Hitchens's criticism in a review of the book: "His main beef is that [she] has consorted with despots and white-collar criminals and gained millions of tax-free dollars, while the residents of her famous Calcutta clinic are still forced to confront their mortality with inadequate care. Ultimately, he argues, Mother Teresa is less interested in helping the poor than in using them as an indefatigable source of wretchedness on which to fuel the expansion of her fundamentalist Roman Catholic beliefs."[9]

But it wasn't only Mother's life that exorcized Hitchens. It was the public perception of her life, beginning with Malcolm Muggeridge's well-known comments about a miracle during the filming of *Something Beautiful for God*. Hitchens makes fun of Muggeridge's obsequiousness toward Mother and comments that this was the moment when "a star was born." According to Hitchens, who spoke with a cameraman on that famous shoot, any miracle of lighting was easily explained by the new Kodak film they were using.[10]

During her life, Mother spent no time addressing such criticisms, at least not publicly.[11] As for the comment that heads this chapter, she made it privately. Her certainty regarding her ministry came from its having been inaugurated by Christ himself. There was no questioning such origins. What she did, she did out of love and in response to the desires of God. Had she replied to Hitchens, who styled himself a "new atheist," Mother might have offered a conciliatory teaching such as this (speaking of herself in the third person): "One man told me: 'I am an atheist,' but he spoke so beautifully about love. Mother told him: 'You cannot be an atheist if you speak so beautifully about love. Where there is love, there is God. God is love.' "[12]

Criticism reached a fresh pitch during the period when Mother was being beatified (2003) and then canonized (2016) in Rome. A 2013 article in *Salon* ran with a headline,

"Was Mother Teresa a Masochist?"[13] The author, Valerie Tarico, could not understand Mother's worldview that saw suffering as redemptive. Tarico wrote:

> By even her own words, Mother Teresa's view of suffering made little distinction between avoidable and unavoidable suffering, and instead cultivated passive, graceful acceptance of both. As she puts it, "There is something beautiful in seeing the poor accept their lot, to suffer it like Christ's Passion. The world gains much from their suffering." Similarly, consider this anecdote from her life: "One day I met a lady who was dying of cancer in a most terrible condition. And I told her, I say, 'You know, this terrible pain is only the kiss of Jesus—a sign that you have come so close to Jesus on the cross that he can kiss you.' And she joined her hands together and said, 'Mother Teresa, please tell Jesus to stop kissing me.'"

Mother believed that Jesus was reliving his Passion in the lives of poor and neglected people. She often made remarks such as this: "For me, the greatest development of a human life is to die in peace with God."[14]

Hitchens used to say about Mother, in talks he gave: "She was a fanatic and a fundamentalist and a fraud. I think probably the most successful confidence trickster over the last century, and responsible for innumerable deaths, and for untold suffering and misery, and proud of it."[15] He saw her view of graceful death and its association with Christ's Passion as simply stoical and not praiseworthy. He failed to acknowledge that this same supposedly stoical view of facing death also led Mother to found the first house for those dying of HIV/AIDS in New York City in 1985, at a time when hardly anyone was ready or willing even to touch those afflicted by the disease. Showing her understanding of both the need to love people afflicted with a then-mysterious disease and some reasons for their contracting it, she said, "Some young people who ran away from home have gotten sick with AIDS. We have opened a home in New York for AIDS patients, who find themselves among the most unwanted people of today. . . . A home of love!"[16] Yes, she loved without questions.

Similar criticisms were levied by University of Montreal professor Geneviève Chénard in a *New York Times* op-ed: "Her Missionary [sic] of Charity was (and still is) one of the richest organizations in the world, and yet at the facility under her watch, used syringes were rinsed with cold water, tuberculosis patients were not put in quarantine and pain medicine was not prescribed. Mother Teresa believed that suffering made you closer to God."[17] That last sentence is at least true: Mother did frequently say that suffering was a blessing from God, as it allows human beings to participate in the Passion of Christ and to come to know God more intimately. She used to say that she saw Christ in the poor she cared for. She also lived as one of the poor, among the poor, and in these ways, she was modeling many saints before her. And the controversies around her and these practices were not new. In fact, soon after the death of St. Francis, in the thirteenth century, there was a division in his religious order between those Franciscans who believed with their founder that Jesus had lived in voluntary poverty, and so poverty was itself a state of holiness, and those who disagreed with these assumptions.

There have been revelations of poor and improper care provided by those who continued to carry out Mother Teresa's mission after her death. The most notable of these came in the form of an undercover exposé by Irish journalist Donal MacIntyre, who volunteered at the Daya Dan orphanage and wrote about what he saw. His article in *The New Statesman* opened with this powerful paragraph:

> The dormitory held about 30 beds rammed in so close that there was hardly a breath of air between the bare metal frames. Apart from shrines and salutations to "Our Great Mother," the white walls were bare. The torch swept across the faces of children sleeping, screaming, laughing and sobbing, finally resting on the hunched figure of a boy in a white vest. Distressed, he rocked back and forth, his ankle tethered to his cot like a goat in a farmyard. This was the Daya Dan orphanage for children aged six months to 12 years, one of Mother Teresa's flagship homes in Kolkata. It was 7.30 in the evening, and outside the monsoon rains fell unremittingly.

MacIntyre's tone is similarly unremitting for several pages, revealing outdated and ill-informed practices in this overcrowded orphanage for dealing with troubled and damaged youth. He tells of being tipped to the story by nurses and committed Catholics who had spent time during Christmas holidays volunteering at the orphanage and came away appalled at what was happening there. The journalist writes: "Rough hands wrenched heads into position for feeding. Some of the children retched and coughed as rushed staff crammed food into their mouths. Boys and girls were abandoned on open toilets for up to 20 minutes at a time. . . . Their treatment was an affront to their dignity, and dangerously unhygienic."[18] MacIntyre compares the orphanage to similar pre-modern facilities in Romania. Altogether, the story cries out for trained medical personnel and psychologists, instead of just missionaries looking for the face of Jesus.

Biographer Anne Sebba addressed this issue in some detail in her 1997 book, *Mother Teresa: Beyond the Image*. She wrote, "Is it an adequate response to take in a sick person, child or adult, and offer care if you are not prepared to give the highest level of care society is capable of? Is it a form of arrogance to make an assumption that, although a body of knowledge exists, you do not need to make use of it?" She quotes a Catholic bishop, a critic of the Missionaries of Charity, saying that the decision of the Good Samaritan who crossed the road to help the destitute man was a spur of the moment act, but if "the Samaritan repeatedly crossed the road . . . by design rather than accident, then the care owed should be the highest standard."[19]

Sebba then quotes Professor David Baum, President of the Royal College of Paediatrics and Child Health in London, to the contrary, saying that Mother Teresa was probably doing what India most needed. "Can India afford high-tech state-of-the-art hospitals when nationwide nutrition and vaccination programmes in the villages are so desperately needed?" he said. A devoutly Orthodox Jewish man who had met Mother Teresa and traveled throughout the Third World as a medical doctor and researcher, Dr. Baum concluded, "It may have been a subliminal decision, but Mother Teresa's anti-edifice stance may be very well judged for India."[20]

Other sympathetic religious people say these criticisms are distinctive of Westerners who do not understand what it is like to care for the destitute and dying in a place like Calcutta. They say that the critics are improperly applying Western ways of understanding healthcare to a Third World environment that is fundamentally different. One such voice is Adam Bucko, now an Episcopalian priest on Long Island, who lived and worked in Hindu-Christian hermitages and ashrams outside Rishikesh and Delhi in the early years of the new millennium. "I didn't hear many negative things about her in India," Bucko explained to me. "I first met the sisters [of the MC] when they came to our ashram. I was very impressed with them and felt that they too carried something very special. They showed up with real presence and I got from them that every poor and sick person in our ashram was Christ to them. I only started hearing negative things when I came back to the US." Bucko says, "Many of those comments were coming from people who generally disliked religion and who were not sympathetic to any religious figures. I also knew how hard it was to work with the poor and dying in India or in the United States. One often feels like one has to go against all the institutions in order to make a bit of difference."

"They showed up with real presence and I learned from them that every poor and sick person in our ashram was Christ," says Bucko. "But eventually, when I investigated the criticisms and spoke with some who worked alongside the Missionaries of Charity, I discovered that sometimes the feeling of family, which we tried to cultivate at our ashram, was sometimes not present among the Missionaries in their houses. For example, once TB patients got better, they were discharged and sent on their way and not really brought into an extended network of love and care, which is often needed for people to stay better."[21]

Amy Gigi Alexander, a talented British travel writer who has volunteered at Daya Dan, has written that she found no running hot water and no refrigeration facilities there. She went there knowing MacIntyre's reporting but also having read glowing accounts by others of the work being done at this home for special-needs children, and she was at the time considering making it her own life's work. "While the days of tying children to the beds were long since over, I often had to do things I was not comfortable with," she writes, summarizing: "Motherhouse provided the budget for only the children's basic needs, and those needs did not include medical care that was not deemed 'necessary.' The order did not pay for things that would improve the quality of life, extend life, or make life more comfortable. Therefore many children had diseases that caused them to suffer, or conditions that were treatable. Sometimes volunteers even paid for medical treatment, as was the case with the child found on the pile of refuse in the street who had been born without an anus. It was volunteers who paid for that surgery."[22]

It is true that there was sometimes a sense of resignation in the MCs' approach that can be upsetting, as if providing a dignified death is the correct approach to every situation. Even if one doesn't agree with Hitchens and his critique, a kernel of his argument often finds its way into descriptions supportive of Mother's life and ministry. There may even be signs of white privilege, as we recognize it now, in her care for brown people. But any suggestion of religious imperialism in the motivations of this Catholic saint who took in Hindus and Muslims and anyone she found off the street is completely unfounded. She did not aim to convert them any more than she aimed to fix the institutions and systemic problems in society that led them to be destitute in the first place.

"I do not agree with the big ways of doing things," she would say. "To us, what matters is an individual." One discovers a very deep, mystical distinction in how Mother understood her calling, and how it joined together theologically in her understanding, when she then adds: "Every person is Christ for me, and since there is only one Jesus, there is only one person in the world for me at that moment."[23] Such a personal, face-to-face encounter with Christ each day was, for her, much more powerful and vital than arguing for changes through government officials or official programs.

Sister Teresa Benedicta of the Cross, also known as St. Edith Stein, did something similar when the Nazis deported her from The Netherlands to Auschwitz in August 1942. On the train with other prisoners heading to their executions, Sister Teresa, a Jewish convert to Catholicism, was calm and peaceful, caring for the children whose mothers were disconsolate because they knew what was coming next. She was a saint because she was able to see Christ on the faces of each of those people, even in the direst of circumstances.

Mother used to teach the sisters, "This is your chance to carry Jesus dying. Carry Him with love. Don't let Him get hurt. Ask Our Lady to help you."[24] Having been trained in Ignatian spirituality and prayer, hers was a quite literal interpretation of what the Ignatian Spiritual Exercises calls a work of sanctified imagination. She used to tell the sisters, "Before you go to bed . . . do you really look at the Cross? Not in imagination. Take the Cross in your hands and meditate."[25] This quality was modeled after great saints such as Francis of Assisi, who sought to take seriously the teaching of Jesus not to plan for tomorrow but to live the Gospel fully in the present moment. In its radical simplicity, this is seen in Mother's actions also in a story in the next chapter, when, in Beirut in 1982, she prays (not argues) for a ceasefire and then crosses the Green Line separating the hostilities of East Beirut from West Beirut in order to rescue handicapped children.

As biographer Kathryn Spink once put it, "To Mother Teresa . . . restoration to health was not the all-important factor. What was equally important was enabling those who died to do so 'beautifully.' For her there was no incongruity in the adverb."[26] And to an interviewer who asked, "Are there fewer destitute people now than when you started?" Mother responded, "I don't know. (Laughs) I could not tell you that. But those who die with us, die in peace. For me, that is the greatest development of the human life, to die in peace and in dignity, for that's for eternity."[27]

Her disinterest in solving the systemic problems that make works of mercy and charity so essential had a flipside when she was also faced with those who argued giving help to the poor because it perpetuates rather than solves their problems. She heard this argument from many people, including some Catholic priests and bishops, but she would refer only to the life and example and teachings of Jesus, who fed and loved people before ever preaching to them.[28]

Why didn't she build hospitals in India, rather than simply take people in from the streets so that they might die with dignity? Those who ask this question never seem to suggest that politicians or opinion-makers who argue for governmental and policy changes to help the poor should also, of necessity, be standing with the poor on the streets. There is a double standard here. To probe even deeper—maybe even into her psyche—might be to find a sentiment similar to that in a famous Jewish midrash on the story of Noah and the Flood. The rabbi sages asked, "How can we call Noah righteous when he did nothing to try and prevent the flood?" Why, in other words, didn't Noah argue with God in the way that Abraham and Moses, for instance, did? The ancient rabbis conclude that Noah's righteousness included a humility that would not presume to question the ways of God.[29]

Mother Teresa had critics in India who questioned the image of their homeland that was presented to the world as the context of the story of her ministry. They challenged the notion that people routinely die on the streets, and they challenged the image of Bengal and Calcutta as places of routine, abject, heart-wrenching poverty.

A single image of her perhaps encapsulates the different understandings people will always have of her life and work, and these differences are ultimately religious and theological. In Calcutta in the motherhouse, on the wall in one of the small areas where people are bathed—a spot where hundreds or thousands of people, surely, have breathed their last—is a small painting of the Pietà (the Virgin Mary holding her dead Son, just removed from the Cross) and beneath it the words, "Body of Christ."[30] Mother said that she was not there when her Lord breathed his last, and so now she sees him in the face of every person in her care. There are those who hear this as a violation of human dignity, seeing Mother's actions not as virtue but only as those of a supplicant gesturing toward a deity. And then there are those who believe they are witnessing Christian holiness at work.

Make no mistake, however: Mother Teresa was intimately involved in the lives of thousands of people whom Jesus instructs Christians to find on the margins: the hungry, the thirsty, the dying, the poor, widows, and prisoners. A Missionaries of Charity house in Rome was established solely for the sake of women escaping prostitution. During the 1971 Bangladesh genocide, when refugees were fleeing to West Bengal, Mother Teresa oversaw MC operations to feed and clothe and provide mats for thousands. When riots broke out in late 1984 after the funeral of Indian prime minister Indira Gandhi, Mother made sure that the MC cared for thousands of people, even working with local authorities to do so. As one sister remembered, "After the laborious work of cleaning the toilets, Mother went to contact the municipality to get drinking water. When it came, she made sure all were in line to collect the water."[31]

Only a few weeks later, when the Union Carbide pesticide plant leaked in Bhopal, India, creating one of the world's worst industrial disasters, it was Mother and the MC who were quickly on the scene to attend to the tragedy and its victims. Their courage and visibility inspired others to join in helping. There are many instances of both children and adults visiting Mother in Calcutta to receive medicines, food, and other necessities, then returning healthier to their ordinary lives.[32]

She also visited prisoners, wrote letters to prisoners, and even created a kind of halfway house in Harlem for teenage girls released from jail.[33] A Kentucky man named Lou Torok, who spent much of his adult life in and out of prison, carried on a long correspondence with Mother late in life. He explains, "She wrote back immediately offering encouragement, love and hope. I was shocked that she would take time to write under these circumstances [perhaps referring to her final years when demands on her time were greatest, and she was in increasingly poor health]. From 1992 until just a few weeks before her death in 1997, Mother Teresa wrote regularly to me and answered every single letter." In fact, Torok's memory had faded slightly: the correspondence began in December 1991 when Mother responded to his first letter with this:

Dear Lou Torok,

Thank you for your letter and thank God for all the good He is going in and through you—especially to the prisoners through your "Care Notes." Let us thank God for His grace which is at work in you, and for all the compassion He has kindled in your heart for those behind the bars.

In His Passion Jesus taught us to forgive out of love and forget out of humility. I am praying for you that the suffering that has come into your life will be a means for you to come closer to Jesus. Let Him live in you, so you may spread the mercy of His Heart to all in similar situations. May Mary, the Mother of Jesus be Mother to you and keep close

to you as She kept close to Jesus. A holy and happy Christmas and God's blessings on you in 1992! God bless you.
   [signed—M. Teresa MC][34]

There are many similar examples of her personal involvement with men and women "behind the bars."

CHAPTER TWELVE

Dogged Determination

"We have sent word to all of the clinics and the hospitals: do not destroy a child; we will take the child. . . . We are fighting abortion by adoption."
—Mother Teresa[1]

When Mother Teresa began her campaign in the early 1960s of combatting abortion through adoption, the Missionaries of Charity were inundated with Bengali children either unwanted or whose mothers simply felt unable to care for them. Mother was delighted to have so many faces of the baby Jesus to love. And as it turned out, she was way ahead of the curve in this aspect of universal childcare and safe haven laws (or "Baby Moses Laws," as they often are called). A similar decriminalizing of abandoning an infant—to hospitals and police stations—has taken place, decades later, across the United States.

Combatting the legalization of abortion in the West, after the Abortion Act 1967 of the Parliament of the United Kingdom and then the controversial *Roe v. Wade* US Supreme Court decision of 1973, would become a consistent theme in the last quarter of Mother's life.

She was, through and through, a missionary. She was always on point, always doing the work she felt God called her to do, without much rest. In the *Constitutions of the Missionaries of Charity*, she had written: "Special periods of spiritual renewal will be arranged ordinarily after 10 years of perpetual vows, taking personal needs into consideration. This will be a period of reflection lasting from 3 to 6 months which gives the religious an opportunity after some years of active participation in the apostolate to withdraw from her labours for quiet review."[2] But she wasn't very good at this herself.

The year 1979 would see the opening of the second and third MC convents in the United States—in the Jeff-Vander-Lou neighborhood of North St. Louis and in the LaSalle Park neighborhood of Detroit. The opening of a new convent in a given city usually originated in an invitation from the bishop of the diocese it was in. A bishop would write a letter to Mother Teresa in Calcutta, and soon the sisters would visit the area, escorted by one of the local priests, to experience the different neighborhoods where their presence might be most necessary. In the case of St. Louis, the invitation came from Cardinal John J. Carberry, to whom Mother replied with a personal message that included what became one of her most quoted lines of all: "Let Jesus use you without consulting you."[3]

This was also the year of one of the great milestones of Mother's life and most significant recognition of the work of her order: the Nobel Peace Prize. It also provided the occasion upon which Mother became the most prominent antiabortion voice in the world. She used the occasion of her Nobel acceptance speech—on December 10, 1979, in Oslo, Norway—to speak on the issue. Some people raised questions about the appropriateness of using such an occasion for such a speech, but those who knew her well were not at all surprised. That speech was designed to use the occasion of worldwide recognition and attention to further the reach of her work.

She began: "Let us all together thank God for this beautiful occasion where we can all together proclaim the joy of spreading peace, the joy of loving one another and the joy acknowledging that the poorest of the poor are our brothers and sisters."[4] She then led the audience in a recitation of the prayer for peace that is often attributed (inaccurately) to St. Francis of Assisi. Her audience was assisted in their recitation of the words of the prayer by small handouts that Mother had asked her hosts, the Norwegian Nobel Committee, to prepare. "Lord, make me an instrument of your peace. . . ."

Following the prayer, she continued, almost as if reciting the Creed: "God loved the world so much that he gave his Son and he gave him to a virgin, the blessed Virgin Mary, and she, the moment he came in her life, went in haste to give him to others." She was a missionary, first and last.

Then she began to describe Mary as the inspiration for religious women such as the Missionaries of Charity: "And what did she do then? She did the work of the handmaid, just so. Just spread that joy of loving to service. And Jesus Christ loved you and loved me and he gave his life for us, and as if that was not enough for him, he kept on saying: Love as I have loved you, as I love you now, and how do we have to love, to love in the giving. For he gave his life for us. And he keeps on giving, and he keeps on giving right here everywhere in our own lives and in the lives of others."

Mother knew that what the Missionaries of Charity were doing throughout the world could not begin to solve the problems of poverty or of how society discards the aged and infirm. Only "a drop in the ocean," she sometimes called their work, which was necessary, nonetheless. But then she surprised many in her audience by truly turning the podium into a pulpit, addressing the most divisive issue of the day:

> I feel one thing I want to share with you all, the greatest destroyer of peace today is the cry of the innocent unborn child. For if a mother can murder her own child in her own womb, what is left for you and for me to kill each other? Even in the scripture it is written: Even if mother could forget her child—I will not forget you—I have carved you in the palm of my hand. Even if mother could forget, but today millions of unborn children are being killed. And we say nothing. In the newspapers you read numbers of this one and that one being killed, this being destroyed, but nobody speaks of the millions of little ones who have been conceived to the same life as you and I, to the life of God, and we say nothing, we allow it. To me the nations who have legalized abortion, they are the poorest nations.

She knew she was speaking to a sophisticated audience of Western intellectuals. She also must have known that the country where she was speaking, like most in western Europe, had recently legalized abortion on demand. Sweden had done so in 1974. East Germany had in 1972, and West Germany had in 1974 (with the law in the latter case struck down by the Constitutional Court a year later, then revised and reinstated in 1976). Norway had done so just a year before Mother's Nobel ceremony, in 1978, after many years of intense debate between the Norwegian Labour Party and the Socialist Left Party.

In her speech, she linked the deaths of the unborn to the deaths of the destitute. "To me," she said, "the nations who have legalized abortion, they are the poorest nations. They are afraid of the little one, they are afraid of the unborn child, and the child must die because they don't want to feed one more child, to educate one more child, the child must die." As all the world learned of the needy people for whom Mother and her fellow sisters cared tirelessly, she wanted the world to know that the truly pathetic people were those who make abortion legal.

While she earned the respect of millions that day in Oslo, it was also that day when the secular left no longer could embrace without qualification the good work of the nun from Albania. Political lines were drawn, and the aim of critics (among whom would one day be Christopher Hitchens) was readied. Though she had already been involved in life issues in other ways—speaking out against gun ownership, Hollywood's glorification of guns and violence, violence against women, and capital punishment—none of her public statements on these topics received a fraction of the attention that those on abortion did.[5]

Mother happened to be speaking at a time when Roman Catholics and Protestant Evangelicals were beginning to find common ground around the issue of abortion. "Her life was an indictment of our shallow materialism and the modern culture of death," said the popular Evangelical pastor Rick Warren, of Mother Teresa after her death.[6] It was as if the other issues that usually separated Catholics from Evangelicals had ceased to be important. And during Mother's own lifetime, this alliance became important to her. She began to meet, formally or informally, with prominent Evangelical leaders, mostly in the United States.

In August of 1976, during one of his large crusade sermons, the Reverend Billy Graham talked from the pulpit about meeting her. He described her work among the poor, how he had met her in Calcutta several years earlier, and praised how she held destitute people as they lay dying, giving them dignity in death. Graham notably made no mention of what Protestant missionaries would usually hope for and expect: helping the dying person to die "rightly," professing faith in Jesus Christ before facing judgment. He also never mentioned the traditional Evangelical insistence on salvation by faith alone, apart from any acts of righteousness, or good deeds. Rather, Billy Graham said to his vast audience that day: "I'd rather be Mother Teresa living in that slum in Calcutta than to be the richest man in all the world when I get to heaven."[7]

Another prominent Evangelical, Charles Colson, the Richard Nixon administration felon who converted to Evangelical Christianity while in prison, praised Mother Teresa in a 1993 book that won highest honors from the Evangelical Christian Publisher's Association.[8] This was not the case for all Evangelicals. Praise for Mother was not universal. Some pushed back on leaders like Graham and Colson. Yet it still seemed that something had changed.

* * *

In June and July of 1986, Mother Teresa visited the United States again. By then, she was constantly referred to, both in the media and by ordinary Catholics, as a "living saint." Her outspoken views on abortion made her a figure who helped bridge the theological gap between Catholics and Evangelicals. Ten thousand people came out to see her on June 16 at Veterans Memorial Stadium in Long Beach, California, at the Rosary for Peace Rally. She gave a simple talk on the subject of Mary's purity and simple faith, illustrated in the annunciation. She led the crowd in saying the Hail

Mary, and she said, "Today, abortion has become the greatest destroyer of peace because it destroys the presence of God, God's tender love for the family, for the life that he gives." She then asked the crowd to pray to Our Lady for their parents, "who have loved us, who have not aborted us, because they wanted us."[9]

These were the days and years of the pontificate of John Paul II, with whom Mother was very close. One imagines that she would have been close, and intensely faithful, to whomever sat in St. Peter's Chair. She was a faithful soldier of the Roman Catholic Church, from dawn to dusk. But she and Pope John Paul II understood each other very well. One wonders, then, what her focus would have been—in a Nobel Prize acceptance speech or on any other number of politicized occasions—had she lived during the pontificate of a Pope Francis. We will never know.

Mother and John Paul II shared a charisma and natural ability to draw others to themselves. He endorsed her work, again and again, knowing the power she had to deepen and broaden appreciation for Catholicism around the world, including among people who might otherwise offer little attention or respect. Just a few months before her California stop, in February 1986, he had visited her in Calcutta as part of a ten-day apostolic visit to India, and the *New York Times* reported the visit under the large headline: "John Paul Feeds the Dying in Calcutta." That account included this:

> One woman cried out disconsolately to the Pope in a language he did not understand. John Paul asked Mother Teresa to translate. "She is saying, 'I am very alone,' " Mother Teresa said. "She is telling you to come back again."
>
> John Paul just took the woman's head in his hands and tried to comfort her.[10]

The Pope was doing simply what a Missionary of Charity does.

Upon his return to Rome, John Paul II was determined to open a MC house of mercy in the Vatican itself. A biographer tells us that he encountered opposition from the Vatican Curia, concerned about who would come wandering in. So the Pope pressed the issue "and a solution was finally found—to take over and renovate a building on the edge of Vatican City State, beside the Congregation for the Doctrine of the Faith but still within the Vatican walls."[11] Construction of the house of mercy was officially begun a year later, and it was opened in May 1988. From the start, it functioned—and continues to function—as a homeless shelter for women. In 2015, a similar house for men was opened at the instigation of Pope Francis; it is also run by the Missionaries of Charity.

During that early summer visit to the United States, on July 10, 1986, Mother was in Lafayette, Louisiana, opening the newest MC convent and speaking to a capacity crowd at the Cajundome, which was then a new facility seating 13,000. Sister Priscilla Lewis, the official spokesperson for the MC, was asked "off the record" why Mother had chosen Lafayette of all places. Sister Priscilla said, "A priest has done things with young boys and it's become a scandal. People are upset. We'll help the bishop rebuild the image of the Church in his diocese."[12] She was referring to Fr. Gilbert Gauthe, a priest in the diocese of Lafayette from 1972 to 1983, who has the dubious distinction of having been the first priest in the United States to face a publicized criminal trial for sexually abusing minors. In 1984, Fr. Gauthe was indicted. A year later, he plea bargained, admitting his guilt, and was sentenced to twenty years.

One year earlier, on June 20, 1985, Mother had stood in Washington, DC, in the White House Rose Garden, between President Ronald Reagan and his wife, First Lady Nancy Reagan, to receive the Presidential Medal of Freedom. This was not her first visit with the Reagans; she and Sister Priscilla, who was then regional superior of the Missionaries of Charity in North America, were also at the White House in June 1981, when the MC convent in DC was being readied for opening and prominent Christians with political connections were evident everywhere. One sister remembered, "Eunice Kennedy Shriver sent people to help fix the driveway and paint. Senator Mark Hatfield donated a freezer."[13] In both 1981 and 1985, Mother Teresa was dressed precisely as she was in Long Beach, with a dark cardigan sweater over her sari, open at the neck. Reagan praised her devotion to the poor in his prepared remarks on both occasions.

Fifteen years later, in early February 1994, she very nearly repeated the Nobel Prize acceptance speech in her address at the National Prayer Breakfast in Washington, DC. The same "Prayer of St. Francis" was invoked, followed by quotations from Jesus about the poor and caring for the poor and the hungry and the thirsty, and then she railed against abortion, knowing full well the position of the current US administration, President Clinton and Vice-President Al Gore, who were both in attendance: "Many people are very, very concerned with the children of India, with the children of Africa where quite a few die of hunger, and so on. Many people are also concerned about all the violence in this great country of the United States. These concerns are very good. But often these same people are not concerned with the millions who are being killed by the deliberate decision of their own mothers. And this is what is the greatest destroyer of peace today— abortion which brings people to such blindness."[14]

Such language might be construed not only as Mother stating her pro-life convictions but also defending herself against those old criticisms that her practices of holy dying were somehow insufficient.

It was reported by some, later, that no one from President Clinton's table, adjoining the speaker's podium on the dais, applauded at the conclusion of Mother's speech. But this is not true. One only has to watch the video of the entire event to see not only the standing ovation on all sides, but also President Clinton coming to the microphone a couple of minutes later to say, "I thank you, Mother Teresa, for your moving words, and more importantly, for the lifetime of commitment, for you have truly lived by what you say, something we would all do well to emulate."[15] Mother's politics also did not keep First Lady Hilary Clinton from visiting her, with her daughter Chelsea, at one of the houses for the dying in New Delhi the following year and visiting again a year after that, during the process of expediting the opening of a MC house in Washington for mothers who desire to bring their pregnancy to term and then offer their babies for adoption. When Mother was canonized in 2016, Hilary Clinton, who was running for president at the time, said the following day: "We didn't agree on everything, but we found common ground. . . . And when Mother Teresa asked you to do something, the only answer was, 'Yes ma'am.' "[16]

Later that year, in the fall of 1985, at the general chapter meeting of the MC in Calcutta, there was an election for superior general of the order. General chapter meetings and superiors general elections both happen every six years. Mother was reelected in 1985 by every delegate but one, which was presumably her own ballot.[17]

CHAPTER THIRTEEN

The Dark Night in Context

"I am told God loves me—and yet the reality of
darkness & coldness & emptiness is so great that
nothing touches my soul."

—Mother Teresa[1]

Five years after that 1985 general chapter meeting, in
1990, Mother asked the Holy See for permission to step
down as leader of the Missionaries of Charity due to ill
health. Pope John Paul II granted her request in April. However, at the general chapter of the order the following year,
Mother was once again reelected as superior general.

Her fierce determination was noted, more than ever, in
these years. As John Paul II's biographer, George Weigel,
explains: "Mother Teresa was not a particularly winsome
expression of a generic human decency. She was a universal
role model precisely because she was a radically committed
Christian." This reputation increased exponentially the longer that Mother was in the news and on television as the
world's exemplary living follower of Christ. John Paul II

played a large role in perpetuating and promoting that image, as well, so keen was he in understanding the power and effect of Christian courage and witness on the world stage. Weigel further concludes: "She [Mother Teresa] was a living refutation of the claim, widespread in the modern world, that a particular commitment narrowed one's horizons."[2]

Mother's courage in resisting atheistic governments and policies around the world and her partnership with Pope John Paul II to inspire Christian faith in such places continued. The documentary about her made by Ann and Jeanette Petrie in 1986, narrated by British actor and director Richard Attenborough—who'd recently won the Academy Award as director of *Gandhi* (1983)—was, to the surprise of many, shown at the Moscow Film Festival in July 1987. One month later Mother was in Moscow to receive a prize for the documentary, expressing her desire to have Missionaries of Charity sisters welcomed into the Soviet Union to do their works of mercy.[3] Then in 1988, just before Christmas, a devastating earthquake struck Armenia, a Soviet republic in west Asia, killing approximately thirty thousand people. News outlets reported on Mother's immediate response to the crisis:

> Mother Teresa said Wednesday she will send eight nuns to Moscow and Armenia to care for earthquake victims in a country where charitable work by religious organizations has been illegal for about 60 years.
>
> The nuns will work with victims of the Dec. 7 Armenian earthquake and other severely injured hospital patients under a six-month trial agreement, under which they will keep their religious services to themselves.
>
> "If all goes well, I hope we shall be able to prolong (the agreement)," said Genrikh Borovik, president of the Soviet Peace Committee, which along with the Ministry of Health

concluded an agreement with Mother Teresa, the 1979 Nobel Peace Prize winner.

The 78-year-old Roman Catholic nun told a Moscow news conference that her year-old offer to send her sisters to the Soviet Union was suddenly accepted Wednesday, when an emissary from President Mikhail S. Gorbachev showed up on her doorstep.[4]

Ten days later, Mother signed an agreement with local Soviet authorities in Armenia, promising that she and the MC would only serve the Armenian people inside the hospital where MC sisters were already working, that they would not hold any public gatherings or news events regarding their work, and that they would make no political statements of any kind. The priest who was with Mother that day, Fr. Leo Maasburg, later confided, "Naturally it was impossible for me to keep all those promises; as a priest I could not only concern myself with the souls of the four Sisters."[5]

* * *

Given such circumstances, and despite her professed joy at all times, it should not be surprising that her courage and witness and happiness were sometimes muted within her. Given what we now know about her inner life—what she experienced, or did not experience, in prayer—statements such as this one now come into greater focus: "Keep smiling. Smile at Jesus in your suffering—for to be a real M.C. you must be a cheerful victim."[6]

She was living in darkness, willing herself to be joyful and to smile. Back in 1957, which is several years after she acknowledged having first lost a sense of God's presence in her life to Fr. Joseph Neuner, SJ (see chapter seven), she wrote to Archbishop Perier, "Pray for me, pray that I may have the courage to keep on smiling at Jesus.—I understand a little of the tortures of hell—without God."[7]

But the world, let alone her fellow sisters, knew none of this.

Three weeks before the book was published that revealed to the world Mother's failure to experience the presence of God for decades, a *Reuters* wire story led with this sentence: "A book of letters written by Mother Teresa of Calcutta reveals for the first time that she was deeply tormented about her faith and suffered periods of doubt about God."[8] The article featured a large photograph of her holding hands with Pope John Paul II during a walking tour of Calcutta in 1986. People everywhere—Catholic or Protestant, believers or atheists—pondered: Was her life a lie? Was she faking her compassion, her faith, her spiritual joy?

The book was *Mother Teresa: Come Be My Light: The Private Writings of the Saint of Calcutta*, edited by Fr. Brian Kolodiejchuk, MC, the postulator for her cause of canonization. Many of the letters that Mother had written during her lifetime had been, at her urging, destroyed. But as Kolodiejchuk writes in the preface to his book, "Providentially, Mother Teresa's spiritual directors preserved some of her correspondence." In contrast to the reactions of betrayal expressed by people around the world, Fr. Brian finds in Mother's revelations of darkness great profundity, "previously unknown depths of holiness," and evidence that "may very well lead her to be ranked among the great mystics of the Church."[9]

Yet there were decades when she felt spiritually dry and bereft, suffering interiorly, experiencing God's absence interiorly, not God's presence. We have read from several of these letters in prior chapters. What Mother revealed to her directors of her darkness is sobering, particularly considering the tremendous energy and enthusiasm that she continued to bring to her work, and to the lives of others.

When she was approximately eleven years into this dark period, which began in 1949 or 1950 and continued until her death, she came to a conclusion: "I have come to love the darkness.—For I believe now that it is a part, a very, very small part of Jesus' darkness and pain on earth. . . . Today really I felt a deep joy—that Jesus can't go anymore through the agony—but that He wants to go through it in me. . . . Yes—more than ever I will be at His disposal."[10]

So, was she lying to the world with professions of devotion and certainty about God while at the same time telling her confessors that she did not feel it as true? There were strong accusations of fakery throughout popular media. Was she lying about being joyful?

Not at all. Catholics who understand the mystical life interpret her experience very differently. The Canadian priest Fr. Raymond de Souza writes in Canada's *National Post*, "The exclamations that mark her letters—'darkness,' 'I have no faith,' 'God is absent'—were not intended as public statements of fact, but rather the description of her striving to see God beyond the comfortable images that suffice for the rest of us. Some reports got that confused, presenting Mother Teresa as something of a quasi-atheist, which is as far from the truth as possible."[11] Meanwhile, one of her former Missionaries of Charity remembered, "Some [of us] had been shocked to imagine that the sweet certainty we'd heard in Mother's prayers had been the result of stubborn faith, not ecstatic vision."[12]

Another interesting response came from Fr. James Martin, SJ, a young priest with a growing prominence in the US media at that time. In a *New York Times* op-ed, Martin explained: "Mother Teresa's ministry with the poor won her the Nobel Prize and the admiration of a believing world. Her ministry to a doubting modern world may have just begun." This led to Martin's first invitation on a popular late-night television show, *The Colbert Report*, hosted by Stephen Colbert, giving wider exposure to the priest's understanding of the situation. He would add later: "A person in darkness feels isolated from God. Yet with patience . . . one can let go of the need to feel God's presence constantly and gradually through the darkness to discover greater intimacy with God."[13] Suddenly, people began to see the dark night of Christian mystics as a sign, not of fakery, but of spiritual maturity and depth.

It would be a mistake to make too much of Mother's experience by seeing it as unique. The obvious example in the Christian mystical tradition is St. John of the Cross and his "dark night of the soul." But earlier significant figures had similar experiences. At least one early Franciscan source tell us that St. Francis of Assisi was on occasion "tried by God with the removal of spiritual consolations." "Blessed Francis thought he had been abandoned by God," at least once, it says, after he performed severe penance to recover from a terrible temptation. "This temptation [and, the context suggests, the penance] was so strong that it robbed him of all spiritual joy." The text doesn't say how long this feeling lasted—only that one day it went away.[14]

Every person has private secrets that are never fully known to others. When asked about her conversion from Judaism to Roman Catholicism, Edith Stein once replied by writing a phrase in Latin, "*Secretum meum mihi*," or "My secret is my own." We will never know all that was going on inside of Mother Teresa. But this brief anecdote, shared by Fr. Basil Pennington, OCSO, one of the founders of Centering Prayer, with a group of spiritual retreatants in Wichita, Kansas, is telling: "When I was last with Mother Teresa in Calcutta, as we were finishing breakfast, I turned to her and said, 'Mother, will you give me a word of life to take home to my brothers.' She looked at me with those deep, deep eyes she had, that sort of invite you into them, and she said, 'Father, tell them to pray. And don't get in God's way.'"[15] Despite her own lack of feeling divine consolation, these were honest words from a saint reflecting her discipleship.

A similar, but perhaps more revealing, anecdote has been shared by John F. Kavanaugh, SJ, who as a young Jesuit spent several weeks in Calcutta working beside Mother and the other sisters caring for the dying. Like Fr. Pennington, he asked her for "a word" before leaving for the airport: "I had asked her to pray for me. She said 'for what?' 'For clarity,' I pled. And she immediately said no, she would not pray for that. I complained that she seemed always to have clarity and certitude. 'I've never had clarity and certitude,' she said. 'I only have trust. I'll pray that you trust.'"[16]

As a final word on spiritual darkness, consider this teaching from Black theologian and contemporary of Mother Teresa, Howard Thurman, who knew a different kind of struggle with suffering and wrote about it as a modern prophet might do, beginning with the cry of Jesus from the cross:

> Out of the depth of that tremendous agony Jesus cries, "My God, my God, why hast Thou forsaken me?"—the most audacious utterance in the entire literature of religion, for here is one who declares that he is surer of God than God is of him, and it is significant that the Gospel of Mark, the oldest of the Gospels, pulls the curtain down on this part of the career of Jesus with these fateful words. Does it mean that Jesus is dying in despair, or may it not mean that in the moment of the cry "My God, my God, why hast Thou forsaken me?" he is surest of God and of God's pres-

ence? For over and over again in the religious experience of men, they have discovered that they are closest to God when in their moments of agony, in their moments of desolation, they seem to be farthest away from him.

"My God, my God, why hast Thou forsaken me?" are words which ring through the centuries, for they say that the key to the unfolding of the mind of God is often to be found in the great inner struggle, the great moral struggle, in which men find themselves stripped to the literal substance of themselves, with no pretensions left, with no props left, just the naked spirit laid bare to the mind of God; and in that primary exposure of radical desolation they become conscious that God is articulate in them. It is the ultimate paradox of the moral struggle, and I love Jesus for this shaft of light which his moral struggle throws across the pathway of all who stand at that point in the darkness.[17]

* * *

Decades before any of those revelations about Mother Teresa's interior life, on June 2, 1989, she was a guest on *Firing Line*, the public television program hosted by the Catholic conservative commentator and icon William F. Buckley. Buckley made his reputation discussing the issues of the day and debating conservative principles with the most famous intellectuals and public figures. Buckley cited the ways that Mother's life's work contrasted "the poor world" and "the affluent world," quoting the Nobel Prize committee's citation a decade earlier. This might have proven to be a point of disagreement between the fiscal and political conservative and the activist religious sister that day, except that Buckley also included in his introduction of her: "I would like to think that I would suppress any opinions of my own that are different from Mother Teresa's. And I propose therefore to be inordinately and gratefully quiet as we listen to her." By this point in the evolution of the Missionaries of Charity, there were 402 MC houses in eighty countries around the world. (These numbers would grow to 517 houses in more than one hundred countries by the time of Mother's death.)

Curiously and perhaps predictably, however, Buckley interrupted her first response to his first question, which was, "Why did God permit pain?" Her answer began, "To give us the opportunity to share in the Passion of Christ." Buckley asked her, "When Christ said, 'The poor we will always have with us,' was he making an economic point or was he making a spiritual point, or both?"

"We have both," Mother responded, "he meant both. And I find the spiritual point much more difficult." She went on: "Because material poverty—if I pick up a person hungry, I give them food, and I've removed the difficulty. Or, if she was cold and I give her a blanket, I've removed the difficulty. But the lonely one, the one hurt, like I find in the shut-ins, is something so difficult, to make up for that love that they are hungry for."[18]

Later that year, after suffering yet another heart attack, Mother asked Pope John Paul II for permission to convene a special general chapter meeting in Calcutta to elect a new superior general for the Missionaries of Charity. This was granted and scheduled for September 8, 1990. It was widely reported that summer in international print media that she was retiring, stepping down. She had, after all, specially requested this chapter meeting to choose her successor. However, when the delegate sisters all gathered in Calcutta, Mother Teresa was reelected, and she didn't refuse.

Throughout the summer of 1993, Mother Teresa again had a series of health problems. First, there was a collapse from exhaustion, then malaria, and then another hospital stay in Calcutta for heart trouble. There were again rumors and murmurings that she was near death. Even her old close friend, Fr. Celeste Van Exem, who was himself very ill, wrote to her to say, "I shall say Holy Mass . . . that you may have no operation . . . [and] that the Lord may take me and not you if that is His Will." He died a few days later.[19]

The following March, in 1994, while in Vietnam to open yet another MC house, she returned to the idea of being personally at the disposal of Jesus in his agony. Responding to Christ's words from the cross—"I thirst"—had become central to her understanding of her life, as well as what Missionaries of Charity were to do throughout the world. Speaking to this theme, and remembering the MC Patroness, Mother said: "Thank God Our Lady was there to understand fully the thirst of Jesus for love.—She must have straight away said, 'I satiate Your thirst with my love and the suffering of my heart.' "[20]

The year of 1996 was one of constant physical breakdown for Mother. She fell and broke her collarbone in April. Two months later, she broke her foot. Pneumonia and a flare of malaria continued the assault into the summer. Then in September, at the age of 86 and with her heart already weakened from two open-heart surgeries, the second of which resulted in a pacemaker, she had open-heart surgery for a third time, in Calcutta, to remove two artery blockages. That she survived all of this was somewhat miraculous in the eyes of her disciples and admirers around the world who were praying for her.

But she was never to be fully recovered. In March 1997, she finally stepped down from her leadership position in her religious congregation. At the general chapter of the Missionaries of Charity, Sister Mary Nirmala Joshi was elected to succeed Mother Teresa as superior general. Mother reportedly said, "Now, I am happy."

A little more than three weeks after this, Mother attended the funeral of Sister Agnes Das, the Bengali woman who was the first to join Mother as a Missionary of Charity back in 1949, a year before there were officially the Missionaries of Charity. Sister Agnes died of cancer at the age of sixty-seven. Her funeral was conducted at the MC motherhouse in Calcutta.

Mother Teresa last saw Princess Diana Spencer on June 18, 1997, in New York City. The princess visited her at the MC home on 145th Street in the Bronx. At one point, she stepped out into the open air with Mother, so that the two might be photographed together, and the contrast between them was striking: Diana, with a beautiful tan in a light cream skirt suit and black-and-white pumps, appeared nearly two feet taller than Mother in her usual sari on the sidewalk before the cameras. On August 26, Mother celebrated her eighty-seventh birthday. Just a few days later, on August 31, 1997, Princess Diana died in a car accident in Paris.

One week after that, on September 5, at just before 8 p.m. at home in Calcutta, Mother complained of chest pains. Physicians were called, but there was little they could do other than make her comfortable. She died about ninety minutes later, with many of her sisters around her. It was her fourth heart attack. India honored her with a state funeral—the sort of nationwide solemn occasion usually reserved for Gandhis and Nehrus. But worldwide her death was almost overshadowed by the intrigue and fascination of the death of Diana Spencer.[21]

A few days later, Eileen Egan, her friend and biographer in film and books, said on *The Charlie Rose Show*:

She took Jesus at his word. He said, "I am the hungry one. I am the thirsty one. I am the homeless one. I am the one in prison." And when I saw her go around in Caligat, the home for the dying, I said to her, "Mother, I can see doing that, you know, on an emergency basis. You pick someone up. You clean them up. You put them back wherever they are and then you go on and do something else. But you're doing it every day. How is it that you can do it every day?" And she said very simply, "Well, Eileen, each one to me is Jesus in a distressing disguise. It's God who's in front of me. And so as I see it that way, I can do it every day."[22]

Spiritual darkness or not, the theme of satiating the thirst of Christ on the cross had permeated all of her life and gave meaning to her Missionaries of Charity from first to last. This is why Fr. John Kavanaugh concluded, "The real story, the deepest subtext, in Mother Teresa's 'dark night' is not that God was purifying her. God was actually giving her her heart's desire."[23]

CHAPTER FOURTEEN

Rapid Sainthood

"I was sure that it was Mother Teresa who healed me."
—Marcilio Haddad Andrino, the Brazilian man
whose miracle led to Mother's canonization[1]

The stories of miracles began long before Mother Teresa's death. There were also stories that, if not exactly miraculous, demonstrated heroic qualities that mirrored those found in other famous saints from history. And from the moment she died, people were praying to her in heaven. It was as if no postulators or pope were required to conclude the process of her cause for canonization.

There was the time, for instance, when she rushed a bull that had wandered onto the street and was threatening some children at play. This almost sounds like Francis of Assisi talking with the rampaging wolf that had frightened the people of Gubbio. And then there was the moment when thieves broke into the convent in Calcutta in the middle of the night, and Mother Teresa sent them away like St. Clare of Assisi holding the monstrance at San Damiano in front of invading infidels to drive them from the property.

Most heroic of all, perhaps, is the story told by Ann and Jeanette Petrie in their 1986 documentary, *Mother Teresa.* The scene is Beirut, Lebanon, during the Siege of Beirut in 1982, one of the worst episodes of the fifteen-year-long Lebanese Civil War. Israeli planes are bombing Palestinian strongholds throughout the city and dozens of civilians are being killed every day. Mother Teresa arrives in the country in response to a plea for help to save more than three dozen mentally and physically handicapped children stranded in an orphanage situated in the heart of the violence; even the orphanage staff had abandoned them.

"I feel the church should be there [amid the violence, to help the people]," she tells a priest, in the presence of two other priests. "Because we don't mix up in politics, we should be there." The priest then tries to talk her out of it, but she insists.

"To go and pick up individuals," she says, is their responsibility. "One, two . . . ," she says in halting English, counting the faces she imagines that they will see, whom they will help. That was always her perspective: not to fix political problems, but to bring comfort to the sick, the injured, and the dying. "You see I always feel like this: If I had not picked up that first person, that first time, I would never have picked up forty-two thousand in Calcutta, from the streets," she says.

The "Green Line" that separates East Beirut from West Beirut is deemed uncrossable. The American Ambassador has been unable to help. They will first need a cease-fire he has told her. But Mother would not wait and apply her energy to a process by which a cease-fire might be achieved. She says she will pray to Mary for help.

"But do you hear the bombs?" someone asks her.

"Yes, I hear them," she says, and soon Mother is on her way to West Beirut. The following day, August 14, the bombs have stopped, the city is silent, and Mother Teresa is at the orphanage, embracing each of the disabled children and, with the help of a handful of others, loading them into a caravan of four Red Cross vehicles. They are transported out of danger, to beds and rooms at the Missionaries of Charity school across the city in East Beirut.

An Associated Press reporter was there to see what happened, and an article and photograph appeared in the *New York Times* the following day:

> Her wrinkled face broke into a broad grin as she entered the Dar al-Ajaza al-Islamia Mental Hospital and began embracing the children, huddled in a group on the floor.
>
> In her blue-fringed white habit, the 72-year-old nun, who won the 1979 Nobel Peace Prize, moved quietly through the knot of children, ranging in age from 7 to 21, giving a handshake to one of the older ones. . . .
>
> Mother Teresa arrived here on Wednesday from Rome after meeting with Pope John Paul II and has been visiting the Spring School, run by her Sisters of Charity order.
>
> "She asked us what our most serious problem was," said John de Salis, head of the Red Cross mission in west Beirut. "We told her, you must come and see these children. She came, she saw them, and said: 'I'll take them.'"[2]

* * *

Mother Teresa's sanctity was grounded in her ability to do, with love and joyfulness of heart, the most extraordinary works of mercy that most Christians would not begin to attempt to do. As is the case with many saints, it is sometimes difficult to hear her teachings and imagine following in her path: "Keep giving Jesus to your people, not by words, but by your example, by your being in love with Jesus, by radiating his holiness, and by spreading his fragrance of love, wherever you go. Just keep the joy of Jesus as your strength. Be happy and at peace. Accept whatever he gives you, and give him whatever he takes from you. True holiness consists in doing God's will with a big smile."[3]

Years before her canonization, Fr. James Martin, SJ, devoted a chapter of his best-selling memoir *My Life with the Saints* to Mother Teresa. He felt that he knew her, in part, because as a novice Jesuit he had spent significant time working with the Missionaries of Charity in Jamaica. His memories of the sisters are familiar to many others who know their work and ways:

> The Missionaries of Charity were always in motion, even in the hottest weather. Up at dawn for Mass, then out to take care of people in the neighborhood, often helping them clean their small houses, then back to the hospice to prepare lunch for the guests, then work, and then more work, and then more work, and then dinner. But despite their punishing schedule the sisters always seemed full of joy. When you asked how they could be so cheerful, they responded with answers that would have seemed corny coming from anyone else. "We care for Christ in his distressing disguise," one of the sisters told me one day, quoting Mother Teresa.[4]

This way of life Mother lived faithfully for a half century. She lived the life of a saint. She was, in fact, ambitious on this point.

Former Missionary of Charity Mary Johnson recalls in her memoir a humorous comment that Mother made to a group of her sisters in Rome in 1994. "Sisters," she said, "I think we should all hurry up and die . . . because this Holy Father is canonizing everyone."[5] She was referring to Pope John Paul II, who indeed canonized more saints during the years of his pontificate than all of the previous popes in history combined. John Paul II played a significant role not only in the growth of Mother's religious congregation, but in the expansion of her witness throughout the world. As the first pope to understand the power of television, he was made to be her partner in the work. His biographer says, "For the Pope, Mother Teresa was a 'person-message' for the twentieth century." Her life "illustrated a point John Paul had been making throughout the half-century of his priesthood: true human greatness is found in a personality that points beyond itself, as Mother Teresa's did in pointing to the poor she served, each of whom, she once said, was Jesus in a particularly 'disturbing disguise.'"[6] He felt powerfully the witness of her life, and that of her sisters and brothers, facing the world's greatest suffering, but with an attitude of serenity and joy.

Mary Johnson adds, "Becoming a Saint was the one approved ambition for a Missionary of Charity, and in this respect Mother was an ambitious woman."[7]

Mother's "hurry up and die" joke was prescient: it was John Paul II who set her on the fast track to sainthood. In March of 1999, eighteen months after her death on September 5, 1997, he waived the remainder of the canonically required wait of five years after a person's death before canonization may be formally considered. He then accepted Mother's cause, declaring her a Servant of God, the first step in the process.

In 2001, Pope John Paul II took the cause another step, recognizing her heroic virtues and giving her the title Venerable. A year after that, he approved a first miracle attributed to her intercession. She was officially beatified on October 19, 2003, in St. Peter's Square by a severely ailing John Paul II. In his homily, he called her an "icon of the Good Samaritan."[8] The *New York Times* reported: "His voice was halting and indistinct as he pronounced Mother Teresa the latest of the more than 1,300 people he has beatified in his 25-year rule."[9] This was the fastest process to beatification that anyone in modern history had received. (Interestingly, John Paul II would die in April 2005 and his canonization proceeded at an even faster clip; he was declared a saint in a process even eighteen months quicker than Mother's.)

Her cause then sat for several years, awaiting approval of a second miracle, which happened in 2015, early in the papacy of Pope Francis, who acted quickly on it. Nineteen years after her death, she was canonized in Rome on Sunday morning, September 4, 2016. Pope Francis said that day: "I think, perhaps, we may have some difficulty in calling her 'Saint Teresa'; her holiness is so near to us, so tender and so fruitful that we continue to spontaneously call her 'Mother Teresa'!"[10] Like his predecessor, Pope Francis recognized Mother's status as an extraordinary icon of faith for the church and the world. There has not been such an icon before or since.

CONCLUSION

The Afterlife

Where does all of this leave *us*? Mother Teresa has her *requiem æternam* ("eternal rest") and God's *perpetua luceat* ("perpetual light"), as the old prayers put it. Most importantly, to her and to those of us who look to her, she followed her calling faithfully to the end.

There are thousands of Missionaries of Charity around the world who are following her example in the work of their lives. Referring to the story in the Book of Exodus when God attempts to get the attention of a young Moses by causing a bush to burn before his eyes without being consumed by the flames, Mother once taught them: "Every Missionary of Charity must be like a burning bush. Love to be true must hurt."[1] This is not easy to follow!

Do we even understand her? Is Mother Teresa, or St. Teresa of Calcutta, someone we really know? She was a contemporary to those among us who are, at this writing, well into adulthood, and with St. Pope John Paul II, she was one of the two great television saints of the second half of the twentieth century. But perhaps her fame is what brought her close to us, more intimately than the thousands of saints before her, even though it is the same fame—produced, transmitted, and broadcast—that built a wall to knowing her in the ways we know less visible saints. As Marshall McLuhan famously said, more as grim reality than anything else, "The medium is the message." Do we see her, or do we see the medium? It was, and is still, difficult to see Mother for who she was and what she did.

It is perhaps easier to come to know one of the saints of the ancient or medieval eras, for whom we have imagined personality and demeanor and physical traits, than it is to know a great saint of the electronic and digital age. In prayer, study, and other means of devotion, we have come to know saints and their ways with God. With much less visible figures—and just about every saint in history is and has been less visible—their "image" has developed slowly over time, and their personality and charism, as people and as figures of holiness, has come to be known gradually in the hearts and minds of the faithful. It will be increasingly difficult to identify the obvious saint among us, as Mother Teresa most certainly was, in the days ahead.

However, on another level, we know a saint when we see one. And what Brian Kolodiejchuk, MC, says is certainly true: "Mother Teresa touched what is most fundamental in every person: the need to love and to be loved."[2]

Acknowledgments

Thank you to Keith Call, David Eades, and Robert Shuster of Wheaton College, Illinois, for help in tracking down details relating to a Billy Graham crusade in 1976; to Mark Meade at the Thomas Merton Center of Bellarmine University, for help in tracking down details related to Mother's visit to Louisville; to Rev. Adam Bucko, for taking the time to remember personal details of his relationships with Missionaries of Charity while he was in India; to Emilie Grosvenor for answering some questions about sources; and to the team at Liturgical Press for their usual professionalism and attention to detail.

Notes

Introduction—pages ix–xv

1. Frank Newport, "Mother Teresa Voted by American People as Most Admired Person of the Century," Gallup News Service, December 31, 1999, https://news.gallup.com/poll/3367/mother-teresa-voted-american-people-most-admired-person-century.aspx.

2. Kathryn Spink, *Mother Teresa: An Authorized Biography*, rev. ed. (New York: HarperCollins, 2011), 31. In 2017, the sari's distinctive design was trademarked as the order's intellectual property.

3. Brian Kolodiejchuk, MC, ed., *Mother Teresa: Come Be My Light: The Private Writings of the Saint of Calcutta* (New York: Image Books, 2009), 33.

4. James Brooke, "Mother Teresa Is Honored at U.N. Ceremony," *New York Times*, October 27, 1985, 21, https://www.nytimes.com/1985/10/27/world/mother-teresa-is-honored-at-un-ceremony.html.

5. Archbishop Joseph Cassidy, "Welcome to Mother Teresa," *The Furrow* 44, no. 7/8 (July/August 1993): 395.

6. Malcolm Muggeridge, *Something Beautiful for God* (1971; repr. New York: HarperOne, 2003), 16.

7. Thomas Hardy, *Tess of the d'Urbervilles*, from part 3, chap. 20 (New York: Penguin, 1978), 186.

8. Mother Teresa, *Where There Is Love, There Is God: A Path to Closer Union with God and Greater Love for Others*, ed. Brian Kolodiejchuk, MC (New York: Doubleday, 2010), xiii.

Chapter One—pages 3–10

1. Edward Le Joly, SJ, *Mother Teresa of Calcutta: A Biography* (New York: Harper & Row, 1983), 7.

2. Tajar Zavalani, *History of Albania*, Albanian Studies 1, ed. Robert Elsie and Bejtullah Destani (London: Center for Albanian Studies, 2005), 7.

3. Eileen Egan, *Such a Vision of the Street: Mother Teresa—The Spirit and the Work* (New York: Doubleday Image, 1986), 8.

4. Gezim Alpion, *Mother Teresa: The Saint and Her Nation* (London: Bloomsbury Academic India, 2020), 9–10.

5. Quoted in Alpion, *Mother Teresa*, 10–11.

6. Alpion, *Mother Teresa*, 117, 118.

7. Le Joly, *Mother Teresa of Calcutta*, 7.

8. Egan, *Such a Vision*, 11–13.

9. Alpion, *Mother Teresa*, 77–78; Lee Winfrey, "Doing the Dirty Work That Real Sanctity Often Demands," review of *Mother Teresa: In the Name of God's Poor*, *The Philadelphia Inquirer* (October 5, 1997): F1.

10. *Mother Teresa: In the Name of God's Poor*, directed by Kevin Connor; produced by Hallmark Entertainment, aired on The Family Channel on October 5, 1997.

11. See Shengjyl Osmani, "Thousands Revisit Kosovo Village Where Mother Teresa Heard Call," *Balkan Insight*, September 19, 2011, https://balkaninsight.com/2011/09/19/thousands-revisit -kosovo-village-where-mother-teresa-heard-call/.

12. Alpion, *Mother Teresa*, 136–37.

Chapter Two—pages 11–15

1. Thérèse of Lisieux, *The Autobiography of St. Thérèse of Lisieux: The Story of a Soul*, trans. John Beevers (New York: Image, 2001), 163.

2. Kathryn Spink, *Mother Teresa: An Authorized Biography*, rev. ed. (New York: HarperCollins, 2011), 8. I say "one of" her authorized biographers, because there have been several; this means that Mother

Teresa simply said yes, often, when someone asked if they might tell her story.

3. Kieran Quinlan, *Seamus Heaney and the End of Catholic Ireland* (Washington, DC: The Catholic University of America Press, 2020). I'm indebted to Quinlan, especially pages 11–18, for several of the points in this paragraph and the previous.

4. From *Story of a Soul*; this translation was used by Pope John Paul II when proclaiming St. Therese of the Child Jesus a "Doctor of the Church," October 19, 1997; https://www.vatican.va/content/john -paul-ii/en/homilies/1997/documents/hf_jp-ii_hom_19101997.html.

5. Eileen Egan, *Such a Vision of the Street: Mother Teresa—The Spirit and the Work* (New York: Doubleday Image, 1986), 20.

6. Thérèse of Lisieux, *Autobiography of St. Thérèse of Lisieux*, 163.

Chapter Three—pages 16–21

1. Mother Teresa, *A Call to Mercy: Hearts to Love, Hands to Serve*, ed. Brian Kolodiejchuk, MC (New York: Image, 2016), 8.

2. See, for example, Donna Trembinski, *Illness and Authority: Disability in the Life and Lives of Francis of Assisi* (Toronto: University of Toronto Press, 2020).

3. Mother Teresa, *A Call to Mercy*, 210.

4. See, for instance, Mother Teresa, *Where There Is Love*, 238, 241–42, 243, 245–46.

5. Mother Teresa, *A Call to Mercy*, 8; Edward Le Joly, SJ, *Mother Teresa of Calcutta: A Biography* (New York: Harper & Row, 1983), 68.

6. Muriel Lester, *Entertaining Gandhi* (London: Ivor Nicholson and Watson, 1932), 13. Kingsley Hall is where Gandhi stayed, in the poor East End of London, for three months in 1931 when he was attending The Round Table Conference.

7. Brian Kolodiejchuk, MC, ed., *Mother Teresa: Come Be My Light: The Private Writings of the Saint of Calcutta* (New York: Image Books, 2009), 19.

8. Thérèse of Lisieux, *The Autobiography of St. Thérèse of Lisieux: The Story of a Soul*, trans. John Beevers (New York: Image, 2001), 166.

9. Thérèse of Lisieux, *Autobiography of St. Thérèse of Lisieux*, 166.

10. Mother Teresa, *Where There Is Love, There Is God: A Path to Closer Union with God and Greater Love for Others*, ed. Brian Kolodiejchuk, MC (New York: Doubleday, 2010), 19.

11. Therese of Lisieux, *Autobiography of St. Thérèse of Lisieux*, 85, 158.

Chapter Four—pages 25–31

1. These two quotations appear, precisely this way, at the top of the most personal document written by Mother Teresa, *Constitutions of the Missionaries of Charity* (1988). This document has never been published.

2. Eileen Egan, *Such a Vision of the Street: Mother Teresa—The Spirit and the Work* (New York: Doubleday Image, 1986), 22.

3. Egan, *Such a Vision*, 18.

4. *Constitutions of the Missionaries of Charity*, n. 232.

5. Gandhi to Andrews, October 20, 1932, in *Friendships of "Largeness and Freedom": Andrews, Tagore, and Gandhi, An Epistolary Account, 1912–1940*, ed. Uma Das Gupta (New Delhi: Oxford University Press, 2018), 357.

6. Gezim Alpion, *Mother Teresa: The Saint and Her Nation* (London: Bloomsbury Academic India, 2020), 181.

7. See Brian Kolodiejchuk, MC, ed., *Mother Teresa: Come Be My Light: The Private Writings of the Saint of Calcutta* (New York: Image Books, 2009), 27.

8. Pope John Paul II, "Address to a Meeting of Adoptive Families Organized by the Missionaries of Charity," September 5, 2000, https://www.vatican.va/content/john-paul-ii/en/speeches/2000/jul-sep/documents/hf_jp-ii_spe_20000905_adozioni.html.

9. Egan, *Such a Vision*, 27–28.

10. *Mother Teresa: In the Name of God's Poor*, directed by Kevin Connor; produced by Hallmark Entertainment, aired on The Family Channel on October 5, 1997.

Chapter Five—pages 32–39

1. Mother Teresa, "Acceptance Speech," December 10, 1979, https://www.nobelprize.org/prizes/peace/1979/teresa/acceptance-speech/.

2. *Constitutions of the Missionaries of Charity* (1988, unpublished), n. 1.

3. In the late 1980s, the *Constitutions* were revised slightly, to cohere with the new Code of Canon Law. At that time, many typographical errors were fixed (see Mary Johnson, *An Unquenchable Thirst: A Memoir* [New York: Spiegel and Grau, 2012], 236–37, 370). But I've never seen the revised/current version. Regarding typewriters: A scholar friend of mine in 2019 wrote an email to the Superior of the MC with questions and received a typewritten response through the postal system. For some examples of Mother's typewritten letters and envelopes, see Daniel Trotta, "Letters Reveal Mother Teresa's Doubt after Faith," *Reuters*, August 24, 2007; online at https://www.reuters.com/article/us-teresa-letters/letters-reveal-mother-teresas-doubt-about-faith-idUSN2435506020070824.

4. See Brian Kolodiejchuk, MC, ed., *Mother Teresa: Come Be My Light: The Private Writings of the Saint of Calcutta* (New York: Image Books, 2009), 44.

5. Kolodiejchuk, *Mother Teresa*, 46.

6. Kolodiejchuk, 102–3.

7. Kolodiejchuk, 105.

8. Mother Teresa to Archbishop Perier, August 15, 1948, in Kolodiejchuk, *Mother Teresa*, 121.

9. Kathryn Spink, *Mother Teresa: An Authorized Biography*, rev. ed. (New York: HarperCollins, 2011), 31.

10. Edward Le Joly, SJ, *Mother Teresa of Calcutta: A Biography* (New York: Harper & Row, 1983), 43.

11. This appears in the first edition of Spink, and not the second. See Kathryn Spink, *Mother Teresa: A Complete Authorized Biography* (San Francisco: HarperSanFrancisco, 1997), 35.

12. Eileen Egan, *Such a Vision of the Street: Mother Teresa—The Spirit and the Work* (New York: Doubleday Image, 1986), 39. On the history of Holy Family Hospital, see https://alrich24newsgh .blogspot.com/2018/12/the-history-behind-berekum-holy-family .html?m=1.

13. Le Joly, *Mother Teresa of Calcutta*, 15.

14. "Catholic Nun Detained in Madhya Pradesh," *Matters India*, June 14, 2017, https://mattersindia.com/2017/06/catholic-nun -detained-in-madhya-pradesh/.

15. Spink, *Mother Teresa*, 37.

Chapter Six—pages 40–48

1. Navin Chawla, *Mother Teresa: The Authorized Biography* (Boston: Element Books, 1998), 216.

2. Brian Kolodiejchuk, MC, ed., *Mother Teresa: Come Be My Light: The Private Writings of the Saint of Calcutta* (New York: Image Books, 2009), 48–50.

3. Kolodiejchuk, *Mother Teresa*, 50.

4. Chawla, *Mother Teresa*, 216.

5. Mother Teresa, *Where There Is Love, There Is God: A Path to Closer Union with God and Greater Love for Others*, ed. Brian Kolodiejchuk, MC (New York: Doubleday, 2010), 213.

6. See Mother Teresa, *Where There Is Love*, 65.

7. Eileen Egan, *Such a Vision of the Street: Mother Teresa—The Spirit and the Work* (New York: Doubleday Image, 1986), 109.

8. Kolodiejchuk, *Mother Teresa*, 120.

9. Father Gary Caster, "The First Thing Mother Teresa Did Every Morning," Franciscan Media, https://www.youtube.com/watch?v= BMmYHmoiNWU.

10. *Constitutions of the Missionaries of Charity*, n. 3.

11. *Constitutions of the Missionaries of Charity*, n. 2.

12. Jaya Chaliha and Edward Le Joly, eds., *The Joy in Loving: A Guide to Daily Living with Mother Teresa* (New York: Viking Penguin, 1997), 15.

13. Mary Johnson, *An Unquenchable Thirst: A Memoir* (New York: Spiegel and Grau, 2012), 17.

14. *Constitutions of the Missionaries of Charity* (1988, unpublished), n. 10.

15. *Constitutions of the Missionaries of Charity*, n. 11.

16. Mother Teresa, *Where There Is Love*, 43.

17. *Constitutions of the Missionaries of Charity*, n. 40.

18. Kathryn Spink, *Mother Teresa: An Authorized Biography*, rev. ed. (New York: HarperCollins, 2011), 41.

19. See Spink, *Mother Teresa*, 38–39.

20. Spink, 46–47.

Chapter Seven—pages 49–57

1. See Kathryn Spink, *Mother Teresa: An Authorized Biography*, rev. ed. (New York: HarperCollins, 2011), 50–51.

2. Brian Kolodiejchuk, MC, ed., *Mother Teresa: Come Be My Light: The Private Writings of the Saint of Calcutta* (New York: Image Books, 2009), 210.

3. Mother Teresa, *Where There Is Love, There Is God: A Path to Closer Union with God and Greater Love for Others*, ed. Brian Kolodiejchuk, MC (New York: Doubleday, 2010), 41.

4. Mother Teresa, *Where There Is Love*, 26, 71.

5. Mary Johnson, *An Unquenchable Thirst: A Memoir* (New York: Spiegel and Grau, 2012), 25.

6. Kolodiejchuk, *Mother Teresa*, 1.

7. *Constitutions of the Missionaries of Charity* (1988, unpublished), n. 35.

8. Uli Schmetzer, "Dignity Lives on as Beggars Fill House of Dying," *Chicago Tribune*, January 5, 1990, https://www.chicagotribune.com /news/ct-xpm-1990-01-05-9001020004-story.html.

9. Spink, *Mother Teresa*, 55.

10. Kathryn Spink, *The Miracle of Love: Mother Teresa of Calcutta, Her Missionaries of Charity, and Her Co-workers* (New York: Harper & Row, 1981), 67.

11. "Director Tells NCCW Value of Apostolate," *The Monitor* 103, no. 36 (December 9, 1960): 11.

12. Edward Le Joly, SJ, *Mother Teresa of Calcutta: A Biography* (New York: Harper & Row, 1983), 55.

13. *Firing Line*, episode S0818, recorded June 2, 1989, https://www.youtube.com/watch?v=3__jvGa5L6Y.

14. Mother Teresa, *Where There Is Love*, 10. Cf. Mother Teresa, *A Call to Mercy: Hearts to Love, Hands to Serve*, ed. Brian Kolodiejchuk, MC (New York: Image, 2016), 51.

Chapter Eight—pages 58–62

1. Quote at the top of the homepage of the website for the International Movement of Co-Workers of Mother Teresa, https://www.motherteresa.org/international-movement-of-co-workers.html.

2. Missionaries of Charity Brothers website, https://www.mcbrothers.org/motherspirit.html.

3. "Br Andrew: Priestesses and Prostitutes, Mary Magdalene—Mother Teresa's Brothers," audio recording of Brother Andrew, MC, at Gracewood God's Farm, Wilyabrup, Australia, https://www.youtube.com/watch?v=-osbDVyRvqQ.

4. Missionaries of Charity Brothers, "History of the Order," https://www.mcbrothers.org/history.html.

5. *Firing Line*, episode S0818, recorded June 2, 1989, https://www.youtube.com/watch?v=3__jvGa5L6Y.

6. Catholic News Service, "Sr. Nirmala Joshi, Successor to Blessed Teresa, Dies at 81," June 23, 2015, https://www.globalsistersreport.org/news/sr-nirmala-joshi-successor-blessed-teresa-dies-81-27326.

7. Brian Kolodiejchuk, MC, ed., *Mother Teresa: Come Be My Light: The Private Writings of the Saint of Calcutta* (New York: Image Books, 2009), 248.

Chapter Nine—pages 65–77

1. Navin Chawla, *Mother Teresa: The Authorized Biography* (Boston: Element Books, 1998), 210.

2. Henri Nouwen Society, "Ronald Rolheiser—Henri Nouwen: A Saint for the Complex," June 11, 2016, address, https://www.youtube.com/watch?v=LytkJkHsfb8. Referring to Pope John Paul II, Rolheiser adds, "He used to stand in front of the whole world and say, 'I love

you, and it's very important that you hear this from me.' . . . He had a huge ego, but he wasn't an egotist. [He was saying,] 'I'm just God's instrument.' "

3. Eileen Egan and Kathleen Egan, OSB, *Suffering into Joy: What Mother Teresa Teaches about True Joy* (Ann Arbor, MI: Servant Publications, 1994), 17.

4. Malcolm Muggeridge, *Time and Eternity: Uncollected Writings*, ed. Nicholas Flynn (Maryknoll, NY: Orbis Books, 2011), xi.

5. Malcolm Muggeridge, *Something Beautiful for God* (1971; repr. New York: HarperOne, 2003), 41.

6. Malcolm Muggeridge, *Christ and the Media* (Grand Rapids, MI: Eerdmans, 1977), 56.

7. Malcolm Muggeridge, *Confessions of a Twentieth-Century Pilgrim* (San Francisco: Harper & Row, 1988), 135.

8. Raghu Rai, *Mother Teresa: A Life of Dedication* (New York: Harry N. Abrams, 2005), 97.

9. Brian Kolodiejchuk, MC, ed., *Mother Teresa: Come Be My Light: The Private Writings of the Saint of Calcutta* (New York: Image Books, 2009), 272.

10. Gregory Wolfe, *Malcolm Muggeridge: A Biography* (Grand Rapids, MI: Eerdmans, 1995), 411.

11. Muggeridge, *Time and Eternity*, xi.

12. *Inquiry*, WNBC, 1971. Available on the Paulist Fathers' website, https://paulist.org/who-we-are/bio/fr-james-lloyd/.

13. Eileen Egan tells the story of these days well; she was there with Mother and Muggeridge in New York. See Eileen Egan, *Such a Vision of the Street: Mother Teresa—The Spirit and the Work* (New York: Doubleday Image, 1986), 237–39.

14. John Carroll University, "Mother Teresa to Receive JCU Honorary Degree," news release, April 13, 1978, http://webmedia.jcu.edu/mission/files/2016/09/MT1.pdf.

15. Mary Johnson, *An Unquenchable Thirst: A Memoir* (New York: Spiegel and Grau, 2012), 107.

16. Chawla, *Mother Teresa*, 213.

17. Martin Sheen, "How Mother Teresa, Dan Berrigan's Lawyer and I Fought to End the Gulf War," *America*, March 1, 2021, https://

www.americamagazine.org/faith/2021/03/01/martin-sheen-mother
-teresa-catholic-gulf-war-240132.

18. "Not Fun Dealing with Mother Teresa," 2009 interview posted by Linda Schaefer, https://www.youtube.com/watch?v=cuddfvaizP4.

19. Diana Spencer to Paul Burrell, February 15, 1992, read by Burrell at https://www.instagram.com/p/B_umtSrjtp0/; see also Sebastian Murphy-Bates, "Newly Rediscovered Letters Reveal How Mother Teresa Inspired Princess Diana to Turn to Charity Work after They Met as the Royal's Marriage Fell Apart," *Daily Mail*, August 20, 2017, https://www.dailymail.co.uk/news/article-4807002/Mother
-Teresa-letter-reveals-Princess-Diana-s-spirituality.html.

Chapter Ten—pages 78–85

1. Jaya Chaliha and Edward Le Joly, eds., *The Joy in Loving: A Guide to Daily Living with Mother Teresa* (New York: Viking Penguin, 1997), 390.

2. UPI, "Mother Teresa Ends China Visit," January 23, 1985, https://www.upi.com/Archives/1985/01/23/Mother-Teresa-ends-China
-visit/1688475304400/.

3. Kathryn Spink, *Mother Teresa: An Authorized Biography*, rev. ed. (New York: HarperCollins, 2011), 214.

4. See Mary Johnson, *An Unquenchable Thirst: A Memoir* (New York: Spiegel and Grau, 2012), 357.

5. Pope John Paul II, Tirana, Albania, April 25, 1993, Google translate, available in Italian at https://www.vatican.va/content/john
-paul-ii/it/speeches/1993/april/documents/hf_jp-ii_spe_19930425
_nazione-albanese.html.

6. "Mother Teresa Speaks," BBC Breakfast News; https://www
.youtube.com/watch?v=xrppvaHZjXs. Mother must have appreciated the work of Bill Hamilton, since he had, through courageous journalism, helped expose the needs of Albanian children in orphanages during the last years of the Communist regime. He also published a book the previous year called *Albania: Who Cares?* (Pittsburgh, PA: Autumn House, 1992).

7. Franciscan Foundation for the Holy Land, "Holy Land Prays for Missionaries of Charity," March 11, 2016, https://ffhl.org/holy -land-prays-missionaries-charity/.

8. Chaliha and Le Joly, *Joy in Loving*, 391.

9. Brian Kolodiejchuk, MC, ed., *Mother Teresa: Come Be My Light: The Private Writings of the Saint of Calcutta* (New York: Image Books, 2009), 34.

10. Paul McKenna, "Mother Teresa, Interfaith Ambassador," *Scarboro Missions* magazine, February 1998, https://www.scarboromissions .ca/interfaith-article-mother-teresa-interfaith-ambassador.

11. Raghu Rai, *Mother Teresa: A Life of Dedication* (New York: Harry N. Abrams, 2005), 58.

12. Mother Teresa, *Where There Is Love, There Is God: A Path to Closer Union with God and Greater Love for Others*, ed. Brian Kolodiejchuk, MC (New York: Doubleday, 2010), 188.

13. Mike O'Brien, "Op-ed: When Mother Teresa Came to Utah 44 Years Ago, the Monks Knew She Would Be a Saint," *Salt Lake Tribune*, September 6, 2016, https://archive.sltrib.com/article.php ?id=4295415&itype=CMSID.

Chapter Eleven—pages 86–101

1. Kathryn Spink, *Mother Teresa: An Authorized Biography*, rev. ed. (New York: HarperCollins, 2011), 260.

2. Spink, *Mother Teresa*, viii.

3. Raghu Rai, *Mother Teresa: A Life of Dedication* (New York: Harry N. Abrams, 2005), 26.

4. Rai, *Mother Teresa*, 36.

5. Mother Teresa, "Acceptance Speech," December 10, 1979, https:// www.nobelprize.org/prizes/peace/1979/teresa/acceptance-speech/.

6. David Van Biema, *Mother Teresa at 100: The Life and Works of a Modern Saint* (New York: Time, 2010), 34.

7. Alice Jones and Jonathan Brown, "Maxwell, Teresa and the Power of Money," *The Independent*, March 7, 2007; repr. *New Zealand Herald*, March 19, 2007, https://www.nzherald.co.nz/world

/maxwell-teresa-and-the-power-of-money/ARX5A6CD6GE7R4
WYTN55TQOVEM/.

8. Personal interview with the author, October 19, 2021.

9. Bruno Maddox, "Books in Brief: Nonfiction," *New York Times*, January 14, 1996, sec. 7, p. 18, https://www.nytimes.com/1996/01/14 /books/books-in-brief-nonfiction-068195.html.

10. Christopher Hitchens, *Missionary Position: Mother Teresa in Theory and Practice* (New York: Verso, 1995), 26–27.

11. There are instances of her responding privately in Mother Teresa, *A Call to Mercy: Hearts to Love, Hands to Serve*, ed. Brian Kolodiejchuk, MC (New York: Image, 2016), 236 and 269–70. There was also an instance in 1980 when she responded to criticism that had been published in a local newspaper in Poona, India. See Mother Teresa, *A Call to Mercy*, 264.

12. Mother Teresa, *Where There Is Love, There Is God: A Path to Closer Union with God and Greater Love for Others*, ed. Brian Kolodiejchuk, MC (New York: Doubleday, 2010), 7.

13. Valerie Tarico, "Was Mother Teresa a Masochist?," Salon.com, April 30, 2013, https://www.salon.com/2013/04/30/love_to_be_real _has_to_hurt_the_masochism_of_mother_teresa_partner/.

14. See Mother Teresa, *A Call to Mercy*, 50; for the quote, Mother Teresa, *A Call to Mercy*, 57.

15. Christopher Hitchens, talk at D. G. Wills Books, La Jolla, California (2006), https://www.youtube.com/watch?v=GZiKAeJ 9mAU.

16. Mother Teresa, *In the Heart of the World: Thoughts, Stories, and Prayers*, ed. Becky Benenate (Novato, CA: New World Library, 1997), 77.

17. Geneviève Chénard, "Mother Teresa Doesn't Deserve Sainthood," *New York Times*, March 25, 2016, https://www.nytimes.com /roomfordebate/2016/03/25/should-mother-teresa-be-canonized /mother-teresa-doesnt-deserve-sainthood.

18. Donal MacIntyre, "The Squalid Truth behind the Legacy of Mother Teresa," *The New Statesman*, August 22, 2005, https://www .newstatesman.com/politics/human-rights/2014/04/squalid-truth -behind-legacy-mother-teresa.

19. Anne Sebba, *Mother Teresa: Beyond the Image*, rev. ed. (New York: Image Books, 1998), 132.

20. Sebba, *Mother Teresa*, 133. On Baum's life and death, see Lawrence Joffe, "David Baum: Pioneering Child-Health Projects across the Globe," https://www.theguardian.com/news/1999/sep/15/guardianobituaries2.

21. Author's interview with the Rev. Adam Bucko, August 11, 2021.

22. Amy Gigi Alexander, "Living and Working with the Missionaries of Charity," *STIR*, July 21, 2014, http://www.stirjournal.com/2014/07/21/living-and-working-with-the-missionaries-of-charity/.

23. Mother Teresa, *Where There Is Love*, 190.

24. Mother Teresa, *A Call to Mercy*, 89.

25. Mother Teresa, *A Call to Mercy*, 196.

26. Spink, *Mother Teresa*, 55.

27. Navin Chawla, *Mother Teresa: The Authorized Biography* (Boston: Element Books, 1998), 215.

28. See Mother Teresa, *Where There Is Love*, 89.

29. See *Bereishit Rabbah* 3:7. Various editions.

30. See Rai, *Mother Teresa*, 43.

31. Mother Teresa, *A Call to Mercy*, 68, 73–74.

32. See Mother Teresa, *A Call to Mercy*, 66.

33. See Mother Teresa, *A Call to Mercy*, 121, 112, 116.

34. The "Mother Teresa and Lou Torok Collection" has been digitized and made available at The Thomas Merton Studies Center of Bellarmine University: https://merton.bellarmine.edu/s/Merton/item-set/31929?page=1&sort_by=dcterms:title&sort_order=asc.

Chapter Twelve—pages 102–111

1. *Mother Teresa*, directed by Ann and Jeannette Petrie (Windsor Home Entertainment, 1986).

2. *Constitutions of the Missionaries of Charity* (1988, unpublished), n. 245.

3. Mary Johnson, *An Unquenchable Thirst: A Memoir* (New York: Spiegel and Grau, 2012), 129.

4. Mother Teresa, "Acceptance Speech," December 10, 1979, https://www.nobelprize.org/prizes/peace/1979/teresa/acceptance-speech/. Each of the following quotations from the speech are from the same source.

5. See, for instance, Mother Teresa, *Where There Is Love, There Is God: A Path to Closer Union with God and Greater Love for Others*, ed. Brian Kolodiejchuk, MC (New York: Doubleday, 2010), 92–93, 102–3; Mother Teresa, *A Call to Mercy: Hearts to Love, Hands to Serve*, ed. Brian Kolodiejchuk, MC (New York: Image, 2016), 115.

6. Rick Warren, "Introduction," in David Van Biema, *Mother Teresa at 100: The Life and Works of a Modern Saint* (New York: Time, 2010), 7.

7. "Billy Graham on Mother Teresa," 1976 San Diego crusade, from the message titled "The Cost of Not Following Christ," https://www.youtube.com/watch?v=Shi9yimphr0.

8. Charles Colson, with Ellen Santilli Vaughn, *The Body: Being Light in Darkness* (Nashville: W Publishing, 1993), 88.

9. "America's Welcome to Mother Teresa June 1986," June 16, 1986, Long Beach, CA, https://www.youtube.com/watch?v=0diqRP9obWY.

10. E. J. Dionne, Jr., "John Paul Feeds the Dying in Calcutta," *New York Times*, February 4, 1986, sec. A, p. 3, https://www.nytimes.com/1986/02/04/world/john-paul-feeds-the-dying-in-calcutta.html.

11. George Weigel, *Witness to Hope: The Biography of Pope John Paul II* (New York: Harper Perennial, 2005), 566.

12. Quoted in Johnson, *Unquenchable Thirst*, 213. See also David Kohn, "The Church on Trial, Part I: Rage in Louisiana," CBSnews.com, June 11, 2002, https://www.cbsnews.com/news/the-church-on-trial-part-1-11-06-2002/.

13. Johnson, *Unquenchable Thirst*, 157.

14. Mother Teresa, National Prayer Breakfast Message, February 3, 1994, https://www.crossroadsinitiative.com/media/articles/mother-teresas-national-prayer-breakfast-message/.

15. Biographer Kathryn Spink is one who says this about the Clintons' lack of applause. I think her comment was then repeated by others, who did not bother to confirm its accuracy. See Kathryn

Spink, *Mother Teresa: An Authorized Biography*, rev. ed. (New York: HarperCollins, 2011), 272. The video is available at https://www.youtube.com/watch?v=kiagkk3XeFU.

16. "Clinton Recounts Working with Mother Teresa," Associated Press, September 5, 2016, https://www.youtube.com/watch?v=WOqlx QpvlF8.

17. Johnson, *Unquenchable Thirst*, 217, 228.

Chapter Thirteen—pages 112–123

1. Brian Kolodiejchuk, MC, ed., *Mother Teresa: Come Be My Light: The Private Writings of the Saint of Calcutta* (New York: Image Books, 2009), 187.

2. George Weigel, *Witness to Hope: The Biography of Pope John Paul II* (New York: Harper Perennial, 2005), 513.

3. Leo Maasburg, *Mother Teresa of Calcutta: A Personal Portrait*, trans. Michael J. Miller (San Francisco: Ignatius Press, 2011), 118–20.

4. Ann Imse, "Mother Teresa Says She'll Send Nuns to Help Earthquake Victims," Associated Press, December 21, 1988, https://apnews.com/article/376b2b34b659fb94298a13dc8b4cd09c.

5. Maasburg, *Mother Teresa of Calcutta*, 134.

6. Mother Teresa, in Edward Le Joly, SJ, *Mother Teresa of Calcutta: A Biography* (New York: Harper & Row, 1983), 108.

7. Kolodiejchuk, *Mother Teresa*, 172.

8. Daniel Trotta, "Letters Reveal Mother Teresa's Doubt after Faith," *Reuters*, August 24, 2007, https://www.reuters.com/article/us -teresa-letters/letters-reveal-mother-teresas-doubt-about-faith-idUSN 2435506020070824.

9. Kolodiejchuk, *Mother Teresa*, x.

10. Kolodiejchuk, 214.

11. Rev. Raymond J. de Souza, "Mother Teresa's Darkness," *National Post*, September 1, 2007, https://www.catholiceducation.org/en /controversy/common-misconceptions/mother-teresas-darkness.html.

12. Mary Johnson, *An Unquenchable Thirst: A Memoir* (New York: Spiegel and Grau, 2012), x.

13. See Jon M. Sweeney, *James Martin, SJ: In the Company of Jesus* (Collegeville, MN: Liturgical Press, 2020), 101–2.

14. Bartolomew of Pisa, *The Conformity*, in *Francis of Assisi: Early Documents*, vol. IV, ed. William J. Short, trans. Christopher Stace (Hyde Park, NY: New City, 2020), bk. 1, p. 238.

15. "A Centering Prayer Retreat with Fr. M. Basil Pennington, OCSD [sic]," Inner Growth Videos, 1991, https://www.youtube.com /watch?v=fM0RRe3miqg.

16. John F. Kavanaugh, SJ, "Godforsakenness," *America* magazine, October 1, 2007, https://www.americamagazine.org/issue/627/columns /godforsakenness.

17. Howard Thurman, *Moral Struggle and the Prophets*, ed. Peter Eisenstadt and Walter Earl Fluker, Walking with God: The Sermon Series of Howard Thurman (Maryknoll, NY: Orbis Books, 2020), 40.

18. *Firing Line*, episode S0818, recorded June 2, 1989, https:// www.youtube.com/watch?v=3__jvGa5L6Y.

19. Quoted in Kolodiejchuk, *Mother Teresa*, 322–23.

20. Kolodiejchuk, 321.

21. See James Martin, SJ, "Holiness, Royalty and Fame," *America*, October 4, 1997, https://www.americamagazine.org/arts-culture/1997 /10/02/remembering-unlikely-friendship-between-princess-diana-and -mother-teresa.

22. "Remembering Mother Teresa," *The Charlie Rose Show*, September 8, 1997, https://charlierose.com/videos/10581.

23. Kavanaugh, "Godforsakenness."

Chapter Fourteen—pages 124–129

1. Elise Harris, "'I Was Sure That It Was Mother Teresa Who Healed Me,'" Catholic News Agency, September 5, 2017, https:// www.catholicnewsagency.com/news/34461/i-was-sure-that-it-was -mother-teresa-who-healed-me.

2. AP, "Hospital Is Visited by Mother Teresa," *New York Times*, August 15, 1982, sec. 1, p. 12, https://www.nytimes.com/1982/08/15 /world/hospital-is-visited-by-mother-teresa.html.

3. Eileen Egan and Kathleen Egan, OSB, *Suffering into Joy: What Mother Teresa Teaches about True Joy* (Ann Arbor, MI: Servant Publications, 1994), 91–92.

4. James Martin, SJ, *My Life with the Saints* (Chicago: Loyola Press, 2007), 163.

5. Mary Johnson, *An Unquenchable Thirst: A Memoir* (New York: Spiegel and Grau, 2012), 429.

6. George Weigel, *Witness to Hope: The Biography of Pope John Paul II* (New York: Harper Perennial, 2005), 513, 819.

7. Johnson, *Unquenchable Thirst*, 429.

8. Pope John Paul II, "Beatification of Mother Theresa of Calcutta," October 19, 2003, https://www.vatican.va/content/john-paul-ii /en/homilies/2003/documents/hf_jp-ii_hom_20031019_mother-theresa .html.

9. Alan Cowell, "Pope Beatifies Mother Teresa," *New York Times*, October 19, 2003, https://www.nytimes.com/2003/10/19/international /europe/pope-beatifies-mother-teresa.html.

10. Pope Francis, "Holy Mass and Canonization of Blessed Mother Teresa of Calcutta," September 4, 2016, https://www.vatican.va/content /francesco/en/homilies/2016/documents/papa-francesco_20160904 _omelia-canonizzazione-madre-teresa.html.

Conclusion—pages 131–132

1. Mother Teresa, *Where There Is Love, There Is God: A Path to Closer Union with God and Greater Love for Others*, ed. Brian Kolodiejchuk, MC (New York: Doubleday, 2010), 173.

2. Mother Teresa, *Where There Is Love*, 294.

Books and Films about
St. Teresa

In previous biographies I have written, I've usually not included a bibliography because it seemed redundant, since every book I referenced was easily found in the notes at the back. But this one is different. The following is more than a list of sources for quotations; these are places to go to learn, see, and hear more about Mother Teresa. I recommend each of these books and films about her life (in English) that most readers may easily find in their public libraries, bookstores, or online, offering a sentence or two for each. I list them in the order in which they first appeared.

1. *Something Beautiful for God*, a film directed by Peter Chafer, starring Malcolm Muggeridge; British Broadcasting Corporation (BBC) Production, 1969.

2. *Something Beautiful for God*, by Malcolm Muggeridge (New York: Harper & Row, 1971). Discussed in chapter nine above, this book initiated the international fame of Mother Teresa and the association of her life with miracles.

3. *Mother Teresa of Calcutta: A Biography*, by Edward Le Joly, SJ (New York: Harper & Row, 1983). The

author (1909–2002) was a priest who worked closely with Mother Teresa in the years before she won the Nobel Prize.

4. *Mother Teresa* (Petrie Productions, 1986), a documentary created, produced, and directed by Ann and Jeanette Petrie; narration by Richard Attenborough. Filmed over a period of five years, it tells the story of her life as an answer to the most essential human dilemma and problems.

5. *A Simple Path*, by Mother Teresa, compiled by Lucinda Vardey (New York: Ballantine Books, 1995). Advertised still as her autobiography, which is an overstatement, but this remains an invaluable book incorporating the subject's reflections on her life, published two years before her death.

6. *Mother Teresa: A Complete Authorized Biography*, by Kathryn Spink (New York: HarperCollins, 1997). Written with the cooperation of Mother Teresa and published just weeks after her death, this is the standard work. Published again in a 2011 revised and updated edition as *Mother Teresa: An Authorized Biography*.

7. *Mother Teresa: In the Name of God's Poor*, a made-for-television film directed by Kevin Connor, starring Geraldine Chaplin as Mother Teresa; produced by Hallmark Entertainment; released on The Family Channel in the US in October 1997. Includes dialogue of Mother which is original to the sources and is sometimes quoted as authentic, given that we know Mother at one point approved the script.

8. *Mother Teresa: A Biography*, by Meg Greene (Westport, CT: Greenwood Press, 2004). Designed first for high school library use, this workmanlike biography covers all the necessary ground but without a great deal of style.

9. *Mother Teresa: A Life of Dedication*, by Raghu Rai (New York: Harry N. Abrams, 2005). A book of beautiful black-and-white photographs with very little text, first published in France. Rai is Hindu and a prominent photographer in India who has also produced other similar books about Mother Teresa.

10. *Mother Teresa: Come Be My Light: The Private Writings of the Saint of Calcutta*, ed. with commentary by Brian Kolodiejchuk, MC (New York: Doubleday, 2007). Compiled by the priest who was the postulator for her cause for canonization in Rome, this is the book that shocked the world with the first revelations of her "dark night." Probably the first place to start, if you would like to read further about her life.

11. *Mother Teresa*, by Maya Gold (New York: DK Publishing, 2008). Another book focusing on her celebrity status, this illustrated smaller volume provides some good general background on aspects of the Catholic traditions and teachings, and aspects of twentieth century history, that illuminate Mother's life. Ideal for younger readers.

12. *I Loved Jesus in the Night: Teresa of Calcutta—A Secret Revealed*, by Paul Murray (Brewster, MA: Paraclete Press, 2008). Further evidence of Mother's dark night by a priest who knew her personally, utilizing correspondence between them.

13. *Mother Teresa at 100: The Life and Works of a Modern Saint*, introduction by Rick Warren (New York: Time Books, 2010). Lush with photographs, created by the publishers of *Time* magazine, this large-format book focuses the biography of Mother Teresa around her considerable celebrity.

14. *Mother Teresa of Calcutta: A Personal Portrait*, by Leo Maasburg, trans. Michael J. Miller (San Francisco: Ignatius Press, 2011). First published in German by an Austrian priest who served as Mother's confessor, this book focuses on the miracles of her life. It appeared soon after #10 above first revealed her dark night. Written episodically, rather than biographically. Includes photos.

Collections of Her Writings

St. Teresa did not, strictly speaking, write books, but dozens of books have been published with her named as the author. As with all modern saints who were not authors, her correspondence, speeches, and talks have been variously published over the decades. There are numerous books of reliable and not so reliable quotations. In addition to #10 in the listing above, these two have been recently published, compiled by the priest who oversaw her cause for canonization in Rome, and they are highly recommended. There is a certain amount of repetition between the three volumes.

Mother Teresa, *Where There Is Love, There Is God: A Path to Closer Union with God and Greater Love for Others*, compiled and ed. Brian Kolodiejchuk, MC (New York:

Doubleday, 2010). Described by the editor as "in some ways a sequel to *Mother Teresa: Come Be My Light.*"

Mother Teresa, *A Call to Mercy: Hearts of Love, Hands to Serve*, ed with an introduction by Brian Kolodiejchuk, MC (New York: Image, 2016). The occasion for this third collection of stories and teachings of Mother Teresa was the year of Jubilee proclaimed by Pope Francis, to coincide with the year of Mother's canonization. This one includes many testimonials of MC sisters.

Finally

Here is the contact information for the headquarters of the Missionaries of Charity:

Motherhouse
Missionaries of Charity
54/A A.J.C. Bose Road
Calcutta 700016, West Bengal
INDIA
Tel.: 0833 589 2277, 0869 700 7115
Email: motherhouse@missionariesofcharity.org

Index